THE JOY CITY POOL

THE EPILOGUE

GLENN BRIGGS

Edited by Michelle Krueger

Cover design by Haze Long

ISBN: 978-1-7369323-6-0 (paperback)
978-1-7369323-7-7 (hardback)

This book is dedicated to my late mother and father,
Vikitha M Briggs and Glenn L Briggs,
and my Godmother, Barbara J Anderson.

Other books of the series:

THE JOY CITY POOL

THE JOY CITY POOL
CHASING GHOSTS

THE JOY CITY POOL
SMOKE & MIRRORS

TABLE OF CONTENTS

THE JOY CITY POOL

THE EPiLOGUE

Chapter 1

The Last Beginning

Four years ago, Joy City changed forever. While it was still the same crime-driven, forgotten location it had been since gang raids left it in shambles, it was different. The city's difference was not to be noticed by all, not even most. To many, four years had come and gone and the city had remained just as awful of a place as it had always been. The change that had taken place happened in the shadows, only to be observed by those who lived in or dared to step into those shadows. Four years ago, The Pool fell.

Those who knew nothing of it didn't miss it, nor could they tell it was gone. Those within The Pool made sure of this. No one who didn't need to know of it was to know of it. It had its time, over two decades it lived before being shut down and abandoned by the cursed few who worked it. Responsible for over three quarters of the city's unsolved murder cases every year, how could such a thing go unnoticed without a single eyebrow raised? Because, it was Joy City, and nobody cared about anything in Joy City.

There was no logical explanation for the sudden drop off in homicide cases four years ago and the Joy City Police Department failed to announce the observation anyway, why coerce a reaction? They figured if no one knew, no one would be tempted to do anything different and the numbers would just continue to fall. They were right, the numbers decreased exponentially. Fewer people had been found murdered in Joy City in the last four years combined than that of a single year's count when The Pool was active. Yet to most of the city's locals, through those years it still just felt like the same old rotten city. They were so unaware just how much safer they had become.

But those who had fallen slave to The Pool and survived it were experiencing something different than the rest of the city, not just safety, but freedom. Freedom to live a normal life not bound by secrecy or sinful acts. They had all moved on, become honest citizens, and cursed themselves for the lives they lived as well as the ones they had taken. But as well as the four years had treated them all, their freedom wasn't theirs yet. Their past was still their past and it refused to stay buried. It demanded atonement.

Aaliyah pulled back her curtains and peeked out the window. The sunlight beaming into her eyes caused her to squint. The sun's warm rays felt good on her melanin-rich skin. She reached over on her nightstand and unlocked her cell phone glancing at the time.

"8:52," it read.

She glanced back out the window and studied the scene below her, the sights, the sounds. She unlatched the sash and lifted the window up. The cool spring air tickled as it brushed passed her and into her bedroom.

She heard a quiet chirping just to her right. She leaned out the window and saw a small bird sitting in a nest built atop her gutter pipe. Spotting her, it immediately flew away into a nearby tree. She gently smiled and pulled her head back inside.

Grabbing two hair ties from her nightstand, she tied her kinky curly hair up into two large pom poms on both sides of her head. She walked into her bathroom, brushed her teeth, washed her face, then grabbed her phone off her nightstand and headed downstairs.

She walked into her kitchen and placed her cell phone down on the table. She had taken a liking to playing light piano melodies as background noise when doing things around the house or even while just relaxing. With the volume on max, she started a playlist, and walked over to the cabinets, pulling out a packet of oatmeal, a small bowl, and a pot. She ran some water in the pot, set it on the stove, and turned the heat on high.

She turned and opened her refrigerator and looked inside. She slightly frowned at the sight of a large pitcher with only a drop of lemonade left in it.

"Really?" she whispered sucking her teeth.

She grabbed the pitcher shaking her head and downed the rest in a single gulp. She walked over and set the pitcher in the sink to begin washing it when she heard her music stop and her phone begin to buzz on the table. She walked over, read the caller ID, and saw that it was her mother calling.

"Madre!" she smiled.

"Hey baby, how are you?" her mother asked.

"Alive and kickin, bout all you can ask for nowadays," she said.

"I know that's right. What'd you and Brianna end up doing last night?"

"Ugh…. speaking of her, Mom, I'm sorry, but I'mma have to kill your daughter."

"Oh lord, what'd she do now?"

"Well, first off, she ate literally everything in my house, left me all the dishes to do, drank all but a drop of my lemonade, and just left the pitcher in the fridge…"

"Yeah, that sounds like her," her mother laughed. "Cut her some slack though baby, being pregnant ain't easy."

"I know but…. God bless her husband, she couldn't be my wife. I couldn't deal with her every day," Aaliyah said.

Her mother again laughed at her.

"Well, speaking of God, I was calling to ask you if you'd like to go to church with me Sunday?"

Aaliyah froze in place as she began searching for an excuse.

"Ummm…. I mean I would but I uhhh…"

She heard her mother sigh hard on the other end of the phone.

"It's OK, baby, you don't have to," she told her.

Aaliyah walked over and poured the packet of oatmeal into the pot of water on the stove.

"Yeah, but now you're gonna make me feel bad about it," she murmured stirring the pot.

"No I'm not, a lot of members have been asking about you though, they haven't seen you in a while."

"I just been…. working, you know."

"I know I know, I just…. I'd be really happy if you came."

Aaliyah rolled her eyes. Her mother had a way of making her feel horribly guilty without actually saying anything too convicting.

"I'll just have to see Mom. I really need the weekends to just sleep in. Working night shifts all the time has me beat. I'll let you know though."

"Alright, well…. how's the vegan thing going?" she asked.

"It's tough but I'm doing it. Took some time for my body to adjust but…" she stopped as her doorbell rang. She was surprised as she thought it a bit early in the morning for anyone to be dropping by.

"Hang on Mom, someone's at the door," she said with raised eyebrows.

"This early?" her mother asked.

"I guess?" she said walking towards the door. She pulled it open but nobody was there. She poked her head out looking left and right but saw no one.

"Seriously?" she sucked her teeth.

She closed the door and walked away rolling her eyes.

"I'm back," she said reentering the kitchen.

"Who was it?" her mother asked.

"No one, probably some kids playing around," she said, "but, yeah the vegan thing, it has definitely been a process."

"I bet, I remember Christmas you were lookin like you were ready to break," her mom laughed.

"Awww man," she said recalling the time herself, "I didn't realize how much meat our family puts in everything. I couldn't even eat Auntie's macaroni and cheese, that almost killed me."

Her mother chuckled. Aaliyah turned off her stove and poured the oatmeal into the small bowl.

"Well, I'm proud of you for sticking with it sweetheart. I'm trying to get your dad to start cleaning up his diet, going vegan wouldn't be a bad idea for him either."

"Hmph…. Dad? No way. You'd have a better chance of…"

She froze as her doorbell rang again.

"What in the world?" Aaliyah moaned, "Hold on Mom."

She got to the door a bit faster this time and peeked through the peephole. She saw no one on the other side. She stepped back and the bell rang again.

"What the…" she mumbled.

It rang again a fourth time and she quickly grabbed the handle and jerked the door open. There was no one there. She stepped outside and looked up and down the street. She looked all around the front door and into the nearby bushes but found no one. She stood there stupefied for a moment believing she was going insane. She stepped back inside the house and took one last look in both directions before closing the door.

She took a single step backwards and immediately froze as she heard the faint sound of someone breathing behind her. She turned around, her body went stiff, and her eyes lit up.

~

Kim ground her teeth together as she sped down the road. She was breathing heavily through her nostrils as she dug her fingernails into the leather of the steering wheel. She looked down at the large gash on her left arm dripping blood onto her pants leg.

She eventually turned into the driveway of her house, where she violently ripped the gearshift from drive to park and snatched her keys from the ignition. She stepped out of the car, slamming the door shut behind her. She then walked around to the back of the car and tore the license plate from the bumper. With it clutched in her hand she stomped up to her front door and inside the house.

As she entered, Rin immediately poked her head around the corner from inside the kitchen. The past four years had been good to her, she looked much healthier than she had when she first arrived in Joy City. Probably due to having shed nearly everything that had been stressing her out then. Her long black hair was pinned up into a messy bun, she was wearing a lime green tank top that was soaked in sweat stains, black leggings, and on her face rested a worried stare.

With her cell phone pressed up against her ear, Rin said, "Oh, hold on baby, she just walked in," as she quickly rushed towards Kim.

She held the phone out to her with an urgent expression on her face, "Cindy," she quietly mouthed.

Kim frowned at her before trading Rin the phone for the license plate. Rin quickly disappeared around the corner back into the kitchen. Kim grimaced and pressed the phone up to her ear.

"Hey sweetheart, what's up?" she put on a soft timid voice.

"Nothin. Just gettin back to you. I called your phone twice after I saw your text," Cindy said.

"Yeah, sorry, I was in the store and I guess my phone was on silent. I was just calling to check on you, how'd your first set of finals go?"

"Ehhh, I guess they went alright," she answered.

Rin came back from around the corner with a handful of wet paper towels and a roll of gauze. She grabbed Kim's arm and began to gently wash over the gash. Kim bit her lip wincing from the sting.

"Y-you think you passed?" she grunted through the phone.

"Yeah, I think I did alright but we'll see I guess. Got my last one next week."

Once the wound appeared clean Rin began to carefully wrap it.

"Well, I'm sure you'll do fine," Kim said.

"Were you still coming up here Monday?" Cindy asked.

"Ummm…. I should be able to, if not, I'll drive up sometime later this week for sure."

"Alright, just let me know what day and when you're coming so I can make sure I won't be in class."

Rin tucked the loose end of the bandage in and pulled it tight. The sudden pressure caused Kim to let out a muffled growl.

"Sorry sorry," Rin mouthed to her.

"I will. Ummm…. let me call you back Cin. I need to get these groceries out the car OK?"

"Alright."

"And hey, call your Aunt Lu. She's been askin about you OK?"

"I will."

"Alright, love you, talk to you later."

"Love you too. Bye Aunt Rin!" she called.

"Bye sweetie! Love you!" Rin called back to her.

Kim ended the call and immediately locked eyes with Rin.

"OK, what's going on?!" Rin asked.

Kim pressed the phone into Rin's stomach and walked past her into the kitchen.

"I don't know much more than what I told you on the way here. I was walkin out the store and these two guys just attacked me."

"Wait, just randomly? Why?" Rin asked.

"I don't know. I knew I wasn't crazy. These past few days it's felt like someone's been watchin me."

Kim's lip began to quiver. She turned away from Rin as if ashamed.

"One of them had a knife…. I took it from him and…"

Her sentence trailed off into silence.

"Kim, it's OK…"

"No!" she interrupted her, "I promised myself, I promised Cindy, never again."

Rin placed her hand on her shoulder.

"It was self-defense, you had to."

Kim palmed her forehead and turned away from her, "All these years, I was good for all these years…." she whimpered.

"And you can still *be good*." Rin assured her, "*You* changed, Joy City didn't."

After The Pool fell, Kim had managed to claim a regular life free of murder and bloodshed. She couldn't remember the last time she had taken a life and she was proud of that. She could once again say she truly valued life and the thought of losing it or taking it from someone else made her sick to her stomach. Yet still, she was a local of Joy City and so no matter how good she wanted to be she had to always be prepared to be bad if necessary; and she knew how to be bad all too well.

"I don't know if I was seen though…"

"Yeah.... you were," Rin squinted.

She walked Kim around the corner into the living room. She picked up the remote and unpaused the TV. It was on the local news channel showing what looked to be a very blurry, choppy, parking lot surveillance video. The video showed two masked men dressed in all black approach Kim from behind as she was about to get into her car. They appeared to be saying something to her but she ignored them. One of them then pushed her up against her car choking her while the other held a blade up to her cheek.

"Couldn't really make you out but I thought that looked like your car. What'd they say?" Rin asked watching.

"Told me not to scream or make a scene or they'd kill me."

She then freed herself from the man grabbing at her neck by punching him in the gut. After a short scuffle with the other he slashed at her arm and she drew back a bit. He went for another but she caught his arm and twisted his wrist causing him to drop the knife. Kim picked it up as the other man rushed her. She jabbed the blade into his stomach and he fell to the ground. The other man then rushed her and was also stabbed.

"In broad daylight, too...." Rin commented.

"Yeah...." Kim whispered.

In the video Kim quickly jumped into her car and sped off. The video then cut and restarted from the beginning. Rin glanced over to Kim as she watched the video in disgust.

"OK, the good news is the video's blurry and it'd be nearly impossible to incriminate anyone from it even if there were witnesses. We trashed the license plate..." Rin held up a finger.

"The plate's fake anyway, there's no name or vehicle attached to it," Kim said.

"The knife?" Rin asked holding up a second finger.

"I wiped and tossed it out the window on the freeway."

"OK, then you're in the clear. Don't worry about it, the JCPD's not gonna spend too much time lookin into it. Plus, they attacked you, it was self-defense."

"That's not what I'm worried about Rin. Who were they, what'd they want? There were plenty of people they could've run up on in that parking lot, why me?"

Rin put her hands on her hips and twisted her lips.

"OK.... well, have you made any enemies recently?" she asked.

"No."

Rin took a long deep breath before continuing. She obviously didn't want to speak the words she was about to.

"OK…. what about any old enemies? You know…. maybe from years ago?"

Kim's eyes widened as if offended by her suggestion. Rin raised her hands slightly in submission.

"I'm just sayin maybe…."

Kim knew what she was getting at and she didn't like it.

"No? No Rin, that's…. no. All of that has been over, that stuff is dead," Kim insisted. Her tone was sharp.

"It may be but that doesn't mean…"

"No!" Kim cut her off, "Don't even put that in the air, alright? It's not that."

"Then what?" Rin asked.

"I don't know, maybe they mistook me for someone else?"

Rin flashed an absurd look at her suggestion.

"Ain't nobody in this city that looks like you but me, and I know I wasn't who they were lookin for."

Kim again palmed her forehead trying to think. With her adrenaline still pumping she couldn't come up with anything rational at the moment.

"Look," Rin began, "just calm down and try to stay out the way of anything else in the meantime.

You know everyone'll forget about it in like a week or so. There's nothing they can do with this footage. And it was self-defense, so don't go beatin yourself up over it, OK?"

After their parents passed Rin agreed to stay in Joy City with Kim and Cindy. In just the four years that she had lived there Kim watched her quickly mature. She grew smarter, more confident, stronger both mentally and physically, and also served as a sound mind for Kim to come to when she needed one, as she often did. Kim attributed Rin's quick maturing to Joy City, anyone living in the city had no choice but to grow up fast.

"Yeah…. alright," Kim said walking back into the kitchen. Her voice told she was truly shaken. She pulled a chair out and sat down at the table before releasing a heavy sigh. Rin stood over her wearing a frown. She knew how hard Kim was on herself about everything, and like most others who knew her, loathed that about her.

"Anyway, I came by to wash my gym clothes," Rin said, changing the subject.

"The people still haven't come out to fix your washer?"

"Nope, and at this point I doubt they're comin at all, it's been three weeks."

"Yeah, that's Joy City for you," Kim shrugged, "how's work?"

"Same old same old. The Drill Sergeant is still on my case every chance she gets but could be worse I guess."

Kim lightly smiled, "Yeah? How is Charlotte doin anyway?" she asked.

Upon deciding to stay in Joy City, Rin lived with Kim for a year and a half. She eventually decided to move out and get her own place not too far from Kim's. She also decided she didn't want to rely on Kim for everything, though Kim was more than willing to help in anyway she could, and so she went job searching. Having no luck finding one initially, Kim reached out to Charlotte who had since opened her own gym where she was happy to hire her. Since, Charlotte and Rin had grown extremely close over the past few years with Charlotte personally training her for free and Rin claiming her as her best and really only friend in Joy City. Yet, as much as Rin appreciated and adored Charlotte, she never hesitated to tell anyone how hard nosed she was when it came to running her gym, nicknaming her, The Drill Sergeant.

"She's good, still workin us all like slaves up there but it is what it is. That woman doesn't get tired of yellin at someone or tellin someone what to do."

"So she hasn't changed then?" Kim smiled shaking her head.

"Not at all. I love her though. She said to tell you to come up there and see her so she can make sure you're not letting yourself go."

"Hmph…. nah, I'm good. I went to one of her group workouts one time when she first opened up, she nearly worked us all to death that day."

"I believe it, she said it's not a good workout if you're not in pain by the end of it."

~

Kim sat up in her bed taking slow deep breaths, thinking, asking, hoping. She had fallen asleep around nine and woken up around eleven. It was now past midnight, and sleep seemed so far out of her mind she couldn't even so much as close her eyes. She flexed her hand and cringed; she could still feel the burn of the cut down her forearm. *Why*, was all she could ask herself. The attack was simply too random, even for Joy City. Rin's words swirled around inside her head.

…. any old enemies? You know…. maybe from years ago?

She knew it was a possibility but everything inside her told her no, told her to reject the thought. Anything else was better in her mind. She had been too happy; life had been too good to her. She had thought herself free but being forced to spill blood again worried her deeply. She didn't know what exactly but something was whispering to her, telling her that the past four years of peace were just the quiet before the storm.

She forced herself up out of her bed and carefully felt her way around until she got to her bathroom. She flicked on the light and leaned over the vanity staring at herself in the mirror. The face she found staring back at her was horribly familiar. She looked no different than what she had four years ago at the peak of her suffering. She was stressed, it was all over her face.

She turned on the cold water and cupped some in her hands. She splashed the water onto her face and let it drip down her chin into the sink. As she stared into her own eyes, face soaking wet, mind in a knot, she wondered if she was overreacting, or was it possible she wasn't nearly as worried as she should be. She wasn't sure who she was speaking to but she closed her eyes and silently asked for a sign, something to tell her whether she was right or wrong to be so anxious.

She dried her face and decided she needed some tea to calm her nerves. She started for the door when she suddenly remembered she had earlier promised Cindy she would call her. Her mind had been so scrambled she had completely forgotten. She assumed she probably missed a few texts or a call from her while she was sleep.

In the dark she moved over to where she knew her nightstand was. She placed her palm down on the right corner of it and swept her hand from right to left. As she neared the left edge her hand hit something light and it fell in between the nightstand and the bed. She cursed under her breath and did another circular sweep with her hand until she found the base of the lamp that rested on the nightstand. She raised her hand up and turned the lamp on. She cut her eyes at the bright light it emitted. Looking down, she saw the nightstand had nothing resting on it.

She bent down and reached her arm in between the nightstand and the bed feeling around for whatever had fallen. Eventually her hand hit something and she grabbed and pulled it up. It was her purple hair pick. Without a second thought she pulled open one of the nightstand's drawers and tossed it inside. She then stood, turned around, and spotted her cell phone resting on her dresser. She walked over, picked it up, and unlocked it.

"1 missed call, Cindy," it read.

She glanced at the current time, "1:06," and sighed heavily.

She placed the phone back down on the dresser, left out the room, and headed downstairs.

~

"Kim? Kim?!"

Kim jumped in place and jerked her head away from the window she was staring out.

"You OK?" LuLu asked her.

LuLu, while still maintaining her curvy physique, had lost a bit of weight over the past four years. Everything else about her appearance had remained the same, from her rosy cheeks to her signature top knot hairstyle.

"Yeah.... sorry.... just daydreaming," she said.

"You wanna take the kids outside for a bit, I'm gonna help clean up in here."

Kim and LuLu were at Little Angels. After LuLu finished school and decided she didn't want to put her degree to use, she ended up taking a job full time as one of The Home's caretakers, which she always raved to Kim about being the best decision she ever made in her life. After hearing about it for six months or so Kim accompanied her to work one day and fell in love with The Home all over again. With nothing else to do she found herself back, helping several days out of the week. Within time Kim had finally begun fulfilling the promise she had made when she originally left The Home for good, to stop by and visit often. It had become a new staple of her life to be there at least three days out of every week, something she grew to truly love over time.

Though she was there often enough to be considered part of the staff she refused to take money from The Home in return for her help. It did her heart and mind good to know she was playing a positive role in the lives of children in the same position she was once in. That was all the payment she needed.

"Yeah, sure. Hey, whose car is that outside?" she asked pointing out the window.

LuLu pulled the blinds to the side and peeked out. She saw the small silver sedan Kim was pointing at on the other side of the road and shrugged.

"I don't know, why?" she asked.

"I don't know, it pulled up right after I got here this morning and it's just been sitting there."

"Did someone get out of it?" LuLu asked.

"I don't think so," Kim answered.

"It's probably nothin," LuLu shrugged.

Kim cut her eyes at the car attempting to look inside but couldn't see through the dark tinted windows, "Yeah…. right," she whispered unsure.

Kim suddenly felt a slight tug at her shirt tail and spun around.

"Excuse me, Ms. Kim, are we gonna go outside soon?"

Kim looked down and saw a little girl with long pigtails eyeing up at her with a smile. She couldn't have been much older than five. Kim bent down a bit and smiled back at her. "Yes, give me just a minute sweetie," she said smiling down at her.

"OK!"

The little girl turned and skipped back over to a table where she sat down amongst a few other kids eagerly awaiting her word.

"She said yes!" the girl shouted as the others roared in excitement.

The sight brought a smile to both Kim and LuLu's faces.

"Hmph…. were we like that when we were here?" LuLu asked.

"Tsk…. maybe y'all were, not me," Kim teased.

They both laughed.

"You talked to Cindy lately?" LuLu asked.

"Yeah, yesterday actually, she's doin good. I told her to give you a call yesterday."

"I didn't hear from her."

Kim shrugged, "Well she's going through her finals right now, probably just slipped her mind. Y'all need help cleaning up?"

"Nah, we got it, go ahead and take the kids outside, I think Blake's already out there."

"Alright." Kim took a step forward and spoke aloud, "C'mon y'all line up so we can go outside!"

Twenty-five pairs of eyes lit up as all the kids immediately jumped from their seats and stood up against the wall near the sliding glass door. Each one giddy with excitement. She did a quick headcount before pulling the door back. As soon as it was open enough to slip through, the kids began to take off one by one screaming as they darted across the playground.

Kim took a single step outside onto a concrete slab, looked to her right, and saw Blake sweeping away a small pile of leaves. Kim walked over and dropped down into a white plastic chair sitting next to him.

"To think we use to have energy like that," he laughed looking out towards the kids.

"Yeah, now look at us, all old and decrepit."

"Old? We're not old?" he challenged.

"You have a whole two-year old, you're officially old. Sorry dude, you had a good run but it's over."

He sucked his teeth at her comment. Blake, aside from a new more slick haircut that Kim thought looked so much better on him, hadn't changed much physically over the years either.

"How is my little nephew by the way?" she asked him.

"Growin up way too fast, those terrible twos ain't no joke."

"I bet, I don't know how you still find the time and energy to make it up here every week."

"This is home, I'll never be too busy for here," he told her.

Kim admired his commitment to The Home. No matter what, whether juggling school, a job, or his now two-year old son, he always found the time to lend a hand at The Home. He was beyond thrilled the first day he saw Kim walk back inside and even more excited when she agreed to come back the next day.

"Got plans after you leave here?" Blake asked.

"Not really, probably just go home and watch a movie or somethin, how bout you?"

"Dad stuff," he shrugged.

Kim heard the door behind her slide open. She turned her head around and saw Ms. C hanging halfway out the door. Ms. C, while still looking like herself, had aged a lot over the past few years. The wrinkles and creases in her face had grown deeper and more defined. It was stress more than anything else. Running The Home was a tough job and she had done it for decades.

"Oh, OK, just makin sure someone was out here watchin them," she said, "You guys eat lunch yet?"

Blake nodded yes.

"Not me," Kim said, "I got here kinda late this morning so…"

"Oh don't worry about it baby, we got plenty of hands on deck, go eat," she told her.

Kim looked back over to Blake.

"You got them?" she asked motioning towards the kids.

"Yeah, go head," he nodded, "I'll bring them in."

Kim stood and followed Ms. C back inside.

"How's Cindy doing?" she asked her.

"Good, swamped with finals this week but good."

"Hard to believe she's already wrapping up her first year of college."

"Time is flyin, feels like not that long ago me and her were sitting in here talking to each other for the first time, she was only what, nine?"

"Doesn't feel that long ago that *you* walked in here for the first time," she smiled.

Kim rolled her eyes.

"Oh no no, that was forever ago," Kim laughed, "I'm old, it's OK, I know."

"Old?! Stop it, you're twenty-nine?! If you're old they'll have to invent a new word for me."

They shared a laugh as they walked to the front lobby.

"You comin back?" Ms. C asked, "If not don't worry about it, like I said we got plenty of help today."

"Nah, I'll be back. I'd just be sittin at home doin nothin anyway."

"Alright, well see you in a bit."

She rubbed Kim's arm as she began to walk away but froze as she felt the bandages under the sleeve of her jacket.

"Whoa, what's that?" she asked.

"Ummm…. nothing, I just…"

Before she could spit out what would have inevitably been a lie Ms. C had already begun rolling up her sleeve. Her eyes grew wide seeing her arm wrapped in bandages.

"Kim what happened?!" she asked.

"I just had a little accident yesterday. I cut myself cooking."

Ms. C looked at her in shock.

"Cooking? No baby, you cut a finger cooking, this is your entire arm. What happened?"

"It's fine, I promise, it was just a little accident," Kim said rolling her sleeve back down.

They traded stares for a moment. Kim could tell she didn't believe her, she wanted to pry for answers.

"I promise, it's nothing, really."

In her eyes was the look of a concerned mother. But in Kim's eyes was a look that begged for her to let it go. She just didn't want her to worry, she hated worrying people. With a soft touch Ms. C grabbed Kim's arm and pulled her in close to her.

"You know no matter how old you get you'll always be my baby, right?"

Kim nodded.

"And you know no matter how old you get you can always tell me anything?"

Kim nodded again.

"I promise it was just an accident," Kim assured her.

Doubt oozed from the plain stare on her face. Kim slightly smiled masking her fib.

"You went to the hospital and got it cleaned right, made sure it's not infected?"

"Yes, it's fine." she nodded.

Their stare-down continued for a few seconds more before Ms. C released her grip on her arm.

"Alright kid, be more careful OK? I'll see you in a bit, drive safe."

"I will."

Ms. C disappeared around the corner leaving Kim in the lobby alone. She breathed a sigh of relief and flexed her hand. The sting was still there. She pushed through the door and made for her car. She got inside and dropped down hard into the seat.

"*Cooking....*" she cursed herself for not finding a more believable lie.

She placed her keys in the ignition and started the car. She looked into her rearview mirror and saw the silver car that she had seen at the window start up as well. She shook her head and quietly told herself no. She backed out the parking space and onto the road and began driving down the street. She looked back up into the mirror and noticed the car had pulled onto the road right behind her. Again, she told herself no.

She came to a stoplight and peeked into the mirror again still unable to see past the window's tint. The light turned green and instead of going straight she took a right turn, the car followed right behind her. She sped up putting a bit of space in between herself and the car until coming to another stoplight where she then turned left. Again, the car stayed right behind her. She stepped on the gas again eventually coming to another light where she took another left. She glanced up and saw the car was still on her tail. Frustrated she smacked the side of the steering wheel and cursed aloud.

"You gotta be kidding me!" she growled.

She pulled out her cell phone and found Rin's name in her contacts. After two rings she picked up. "Hey," she answered.

Kim put the phone on speaker and placed it on the center console as she continued to drive. "Hey, where are you?"

"Bout to walk out the house, what's up?"

"Don't leave," Kim told her.

"What?"

"Don't leave, I'll be at your house in like five minutes."

"Kim, I gotta be at work at…"

"Rin!" she huffed, "Listen to me, do not leave. I'll be there in five minutes. Be outside when I get there."

She heard her sigh heavily into the phone. She could practically feel her rolling her eyes.

"Alright, can you at least tell me…"

Kim hung up on her before she could finish her sentence. She slid her phone back into her pocket and took a small detour on the way to Rin's house full of unnecessary turns. The car mirrored every move she made. There was no question it was following her.

She eventually pulled into the driveway of Rin's small but comfortable home. Kim quickly stepped out the car as Rin stepped out from behind her storm door onto the porch. She had a small duffle bag hanging off one of her shoulders. They met halfway in between the car and house.

"What's up…"

"Silver car pullin up now," Kim whispered as she walked into Rin pushing her along.

"What?"

Rin looked over her shoulder towards the street but Kim quickly nudged her.

"Don't look, it followed me here and up to The Home this morning."

The two of them made for the side of the house leading into the backyard.

"Did you see who was in it?" she asked.

"No."

"You think they might have something to do with…"

"I don't know," she cut her off.

They walked in between the side of Rin's house and the fence that separated it from her neighbor. They came to the backyard and Kim moved around the corner out of sight pressing her back against the house. She pulled Rin right next to her.

"Ummm…. is there a plan I should know about?" Rin asked.

Kim hushed her as she listened carefully. A car door slammed shut. Then it was quiet. Then the sound of someone slowly walking in the grass, inching closer caught both of their ears. Kim grabbed the charm of her chain and tucked it into her shirt. She turned to Rin who gently nodded at her. Kim stepped out from around the corner and stood motionless. Her follower froze at the sight of her.

She looked the person up and down. Their build looked to be that of a man. He was about her same height but more muscular. Masked and dressed in all black, he reminded Kim too much of the men who had attacked her the day before; it was unnerving.

"You been followin me all day. Do we have a problem?" Kim asked.

Suddenly the man fell into a sprint towards Kim. She took a few steps back and widened her stance ready to defend herself. Just as he passed the corner of the house Rin grabbed him by his collar and jerked him towards her. She stuck a knife into his chest, pulled it out, and then stuck it in his gut. She twisted it before pulling it out and pushed the man over onto the ground. Kim winced at the sight.

Watching someone be stabbed up close was something she hadn't experienced in a while.

"Welp, he's dead now, or he will be soon, problem solved," Rin said.

Rin on the other hand seemed indifferent to the murder she had just committed. A far cry from how the act once triggered her in the past. It was obvious living in Joy City for four years had had an effect on her; she was much tougher and had befriended an ex-assassin.

"Look familiar?" Rin asked, "Anything like the guys that attacked you yesterday?"

Kim stood over the man and pulled his mask down. She didn't recognize him.

"I mean, the dark clothing yeah, but that's not uncommon in Joy City."

She looked his body over and noticed a bulging pocket on the jacket he was wearing. She patted it and found it was solid. She opened the pocket and pulled out a black rectangular shaped device. It had a small square display screen near the top, a round silver button in the middle, and several speaker holes towards the bottom. Kim looked it over puzzled.

"Is that a.... voice recorder?" Rin asked.

Kim looked at the silver button and noticed a small right facing triangle in the center of it. She pressed the button and the small screen lit up blue as a recording began playing.

"Kim, if you're listening to this then that means everything that I believe to know about you is true."

It was a man's voice speaking, he sounded old. He spoke slowly, enunciating every word through a southern accent accompanied by a small lisp. Every S and C he spoke was held as though he were a serpent.

"You don't know me, but I know you oh so well. Knew your parents even better, the ones who took you in that is. You know what this is, you know what this is about. And in time, you'll suffer for all of it."

The recording ended and the screen went black. Kim could only stare at the device mystified. The voice sounded evil; its words were so condemning. She had absolutely no clue who or what she had just listened to.

Rin placed her hand on her waist and sighed.

"Uhhh…. Kim, I know you're tryin to leave it all behind you but that," she pointed to the device, "that was wild. I really think you should go see…"

"Go pack everything you need to last a few days," Kim said.

"What?" Rin asked.

"Whatever you need to make it the next few days, you're not staying in this house."

"Why…"

"Because whoever this is now knows where this house is and we're not taking any chances."

"So what we're going to your house?" she asked.

"No, my house is probably hotter than here."

"Then where are we…"

"I'm gonna make a call," Kim said pulling her cell phone out.

She began frantically swiping and tapping on the screen.

"Kim, I gotta get to work," Rin pleaded.

"You can call Charlotte later, go pack!" Kim commanded her.

Rin rolled her eyes and scoffed as she started to walk back towards the front of the house.

"Can you at least get this jerk off my lawn?" she said stepping over the man's body.

"I'll handle it," Kim said pressing her phone up to her cheek.

It rang three times before the call was picked up.

"Hello?" a soft voice answered.

The curiosity in the voice told they were a bit surprised by her call.

"Hey, are you home?" Kim asked.

"Yeah, what's up?"

"We gotta talk, me and Rin are on the way, we'll be there in ten."

Chapter 2

Relapse

Kim pulled her car into the driveway of a bright yellow two-story home. She stepped out the car and quickly assessed her surroundings before beginning to walk up to the front door. Rin followed closely behind her. Once in front of the door Kim rang the doorbell. They could hear the chimes inside from where they stood. After a few seconds of waiting, they began to hear motion on the other side as the locks were turned and the door swung open. Kim gently smiled as she looked upon a friendly face she hadn't seen in a while. One that looked just as happy and healthy as it had four years ago.

"Hey," she grinned.

"Long time no see," Aaliyah smiled back.

She grabbed Kim's hand and pulled her in for a tight hug. She released her and let her walk by and into the house, then traded smiles with Rin.

"Hey girl," she said extending out her fist which Rin met with her own as she entered the house as well.

Aaliyah leaned outside and took a quick gaze up and down the street before closing the door.

Kim dropped down onto the couch in the living room. She lazily slumped down into the cushion. Rin propped herself up against the wall.

"Y'all look beat," Aaliyah said joining them in the living room, "JC ain't been kind to you lately?"

Unlike Kim and Charlotte, after the fall of The Pool Aaliyah didn't start a business, didn't get a job, or decide to volunteer anywhere. She had invested her money so that it turned over for her indefinitely, she was essentially set for life. With that freedom she simply chose to just live her life. Whether that meant taking month-long vacations out of the country, learning a new hobby to then drop it the following week for a new one, or simply watching TV all day until she became too tired to continue looking at the screen. She just lived day to day, relishing in the ability to do whatever she wanted, whenever she wanted, and however she wanted.

Though Kim hadn't completely lost contact with Aaliyah, she could hardly remember the last time she had seen or spoken to her. There was no reason for their lack of contact other than without The Pool they simply didn't have much to talk about or much in common. They were just two people living in the same city again. Yet, even though they hadn't heard from each other much over the past four years, they had still been through too much together to not consider each other family.

"Ummm…. you here alone?" Kim asked scanning the room.

"Yeah, it's just me," Aaliyah answered.

Kim sat up straight and looked hard at her.

"What's up?" Aaliyah asked looking between her and Rin.

"I-I think I'm being hunted," Kim told her.

She struggled to get the words past her lips as if she wasn't quite sure of what she was even saying. Aaliyah's eyes grew big. She looked over to Rin who could only shrug as she leaned up against the wall.

"OK…. you have my attention, go on" Aaliyah said.

"I don't really know. Yesterday two guys attacked me in the parking lot of the grocery store. Today someone followed me from my house up to Little Angels, waited for me to leave, and then followed me to Rin's house. Had to kill all three." Kim's voice shrunk a bit as she spoke the men's fates.

"Assassins?" Aaliyah asked.

"Doubt it, barely a step above street thugs," Kim said.

"How do you know you're being hunted then? I mean is it possible it was just two random…"

"Nah, there's no such thing as coincidences," Rin interrupted, "I know we're talkin about Joy City but two attacks on the same person on back to back days, nah, there's nothin random about that."

"And then there's this…." Kim added removing the voice recorder from her pocket.

"What's that?" Aaliyah asked.

Kim pressed the play button.

"Kim, if you're listening to this then that means everything that I believe to know about you is true. You don't know me, but I know you oh so well. Knew your parents even better, the ones who took you in that is. You know what this is, you know what this is about."

Aaliyah stared at the device with a mix of confusion and disgust as she listened. Kim caught chills listening to the voice again.

"And in time, you'll suffer for all of it."

Aaliyah's worrisome gaze rose and met Kim's.

"OK, so…. I'm guessing we don't know who this is?"

"No clue," Kim shook her head, "don't know how he seems to know me or what his problem with me is either."

"Really?" Rin stepped forward, "Kim, you know, you don't wanna admit it, but you know."

Kim rolled her eyes at her.

Rin turned her attention to Aaliyah, "What do you think it is?" Rin asked her. Sarcasm bled from her tone. "What reason would a person have to have a vendetta against her? What has she done in her life that might make someone believe she deserves to *suffer?*"

Kim pressed her lips together into a frown annoyed by Rin's picking.

"Ummm…." Aaliyah gnawed on the inside of her cheek as she appeared to be lost in thought, "I…. let me show y'all somethin."

She stood and Kim and Rin followed her over to a door in her hallway. She opened the door and inside it was pitch black. She flicked on a light and it revealed a flight of wooden stairs heading down.

"Watch your step," Aaliyah called over her shoulder as she started down.

Kim and Rin followed behind her closely. They both turned their noses up as a rancid smell hit their nostrils.

"Thursday, I woke up, started my day or whatever, and my doorbell rang. I went to see who it was and no one was there."

As she got to the bottom of the stairs she flicked on another switch that lit the entire basement. It was a moderately sized basement that appeared to be used for nothing more than storage. A couple of boxes, filled trash bags, and old pieces of furniture lined the walls. In the center of the floor was a tall wooden table standing about waist tall. Resting on the table was a black body bag. Kim's heart skipped a beat at the sight of it.

"Didn't think anything of it until it rang again," Aaliyah continued walking over towards the table, "but when I looked there was still no one there."

She grabbed the zipper and began pulling it down.

"I stepped outside expecting to see some kids running away or somethin but nothin. Got back inside, turned around, and this fool attacked me."

She stopped the zipper halfway down and opened the bag for Kim and Rin to see a masked man dressed in black lying inside. Kim immediately noticed several punctures in his clothes.

"So, do you keep the dead bodies of everyone you kill as trophies?" Rin teased.

"He's only down here cause I didn't really have a better option. I wasn't planning on having to get rid of a body that morning." Aaliyah turned to Kim, "It might be a long shot but you think the attacks might be related?"

"It's not a long shot. It's actually the only thing that makes sense when you think about it," Rin argued.

They both turned to Kim. Her eyes were still on the body. She examined it up and down thoroughly.

"Did you find anything on him?" Kim asked.

"Didn't look actually. I brought him down here, put him in the bag, and just started thinkin of places to dump him," Aaliyah said.

Kim unzipped the bag down a little more and began frisking the body until she felt something in one of the man's pockets. She reached inside and pulled out a voice recorder identical to the one she had found on the man Rin killed earlier.

"Tsk.... are the attacks related?" Rin mocked Aaliyah's words.

Kim pressed the silver play button and the recording began.

"Aaliyah," the same voice from the other recording sighed, *"life has been so kind to you these past few years hasn't it? No job, no responsibilities, no obligations, free from what enslaved you for so long. But what got you here? Sin. A whole lotta sin."*

Aaliyah's face turned as she listened.

"*And you will answer for those sins, every single one.*"

The recording ended, leaving the three of them standing in silence. Kim looked to Aaliyah but she refused to look back at her. She shook her head slowly as she stared down at the table.

"OK…. I thought it was possible it had something to do with…. but I didn't wanna rile anyone up, I didn't wanna bother y'all, so I let it go. Thought maybe it was just a random break-in, but…. but that…"

"Isn't debatable," Rin finished her sentence. She looked over to Kim.

"Do you need to hear anything else?" Rin asked.

Kim dropped the recorder on the table and turned her back to them both. She took a few steps away and squeezed her head in between her hands.

"Four years!" she groaned, "Four years free and this just shows up outta nowhere?!"

"We did a lotta dirt before we got free," Aaliyah reminded her, "it's not surprising we upset someone."

"No one knew what we were doing though," Kim protested.

"Well, whoever this is does," Aaliyah said pointing at the recorder, "so what now?"

Kim paused for a moment to think.

"Look," Rin began, "I understand neither of you wanna call it what it is but at this point we really need to go see…"

"Charlotte," Kim interrupted her.

"What?" Rin side eyed her.

"Yeah, if this is what we think someone'll be coming after her pretty soon too, if they haven't already been sent," Aaliyah said.

"Have you heard from her lately?" Kim asked her.

Aaliyah shook her head no, "I don't remember the last time I even talked to her on the phone. The last time I actually saw her was the day she tried to kill us at that workout session a few years back."

Kim looked over to Rin.

"Has she said anything to you about an attack, anyone following her?"

"Nah."

"Do you know where she is right now?"

"At the gym, I'm sure."

"Can you call her?"

"Saturdays are busy, she's not gonna have her phone on her."

"Then we need to go, now," Kim said eyeing them both.

"Can we find somewhere to dump him on the way before he starts stinkin up my entire house?" Aaliyah asked pointing to the body.

"Yeah, zip him up," Kim said.

~

Kim, Rin, and Aaliyah arrived at Charlotte's gym. It was packed just as Rin said it would be. As the three of them walked up to the building Kim shook her head as she read the name posted above the building's main entrance.

"Wellness Pool," it read.

"Can't tell if she thought it was funny or if she just wanted to taunt the life she used to live when she named this place," Kim whispered to Aaliyah.

They walked inside and were blasted with a gust of cold air. Kim quickly scanned around and saw aside from a few pieces of equipment misplaced inside the gym looked exactly as she had remembered it. It was a two-story building, cream-colored walls with a lime green strip running through the middle. In the middle of the floor there were numerous pieces of exercise equipment all neatly separated into specific zones. To the far right behind a window of glass was a large pool used for water aerobics classes and two dance studio rooms. Straight back behind a set of double doors were two full sized basketball courts. To the far left a small counter serving smoothies and sports drinks. Right next to it was a room dedicated for small children to play in while their parents exercised. And this was just the bottom floor, from what Kim remembered the second floor had even more.

Charlotte had dumped millions into the place and every penny seemed to be paying off. From the day it first opened the gym thrived, becoming one of the most successful private businesses to ever start in Joy City. Kim was happy for Charlotte to have found something honest she could pour her heart into that also helped so many people.

"Hey Rin!" an Asian woman standing behind the front desk happily greeted her.

The three of them approached the desk with Rin in front.

"Hey Hannah."

"Thought you weren't comin in today," the girl said.

"Yeah, well I'm not actually here to work right now," Rin said leaning over the desk.

"Then you better get outta here," the girl laughed, "Charlotte's already upset you didn't show up this morning. She's already threatened to kill you three times today."

"Only three? Huh.... guess she's in a good mood today."

The girl laughed.

"Hey?" Kim gently tapped Rin's shoulder growing impatient.

"Ummm.... speaking of her, where is she?" Rin asked.

"She just started her calisthenics class," she said pointing to one of the dance studios.

They all looked over and saw Charlotte standing in front of a group of about fifteen other women. They were all following her in a series of stretching exercises. Kim stepped forward.

"We just need to speak to her really quickly," she said to the girl.

"Once she gets going teaching there's no stopping her until she's done," she shrugged. "you're welcome to stay and talk to her after she finishes though."

43

"How long will that be?" Kim asked.

"Well, they just started so probably about another hour and a half."

Kim sucked her teeth.

"It's fine," Rin said, "when she finishes up can you just tell her to give me a call ASAP?"

"Will do," she smiled.

"Thanks Hannah, I'll see you Monday."

"Alright see you."

They all turned and headed back outside. Kim looked to Rin.

"Text her and tell her to meet us at Aaliyah's as soon as she can."

"Should we leave?" Aaliyah asked, "I mean realistically, if someone's coming after her a lot of people could be put in danger if they go runnin up in there."

"She's got security, plus I don't think they will. The two that attacked me at the store waited for me to get to my car, and the guy who followed me from home waited for me to leave Little Angels before even trying to attack. It seems like whoever this is isn't trying to hurt anyone but us."

"But are you sure of that?" Aaliyah asked.

Kim thought for a moment before answering.

She shook her head and answered, "No."

~

"I was gonna come back but I ended up waiting forever to get food and then Rin called me and told me she needed a ride to work."

Kim sat on the floor of Aaliyah's living room on the phone with LuLu explaining why she hadn't come back to The Home yet. Without The Pool, Kim had found herself able to be a lot more truthful with everyone she dealt with regularly. She no longer felt like she had to create false alibis or tell of conversations and happenings that never were. To find herself having to do so again both hurt and scared her.

"Oh, OK. Well, Ms. C just asked me to check on you," LuLu said.

"She's not mad is she?" Kim asked.

"No, of course not, she was just worried."

Rin poked her head around the corner and held her cell phone up beckoning for Kim's attention.

"Alright. Well hey Lu, let me go I gotta.... ummm...." Kim froze unable to find a quick lie, she was so out of practice. ".... I-I told Cindy I'd give her a call," she finally mustered.

"Oh, OK. Well, tell her I said hey?"

"Yeah.... I will. I'll see you soon," Kim said.

She hung up and dropped her head in shame.

"Let's hope you don't end up in an interrogation room anytime soon, you'll get ate up," Rin teased.

Kim sighed ignoring her comment.

"What's up?" she asked.

"Charlotte just texted me, she said she's gotta go pick her parents up from the airport tonight after she gets off."

"When does she get off?" Kim asked.

"In like five hours."

"Five hours? That'll be like nine, the airports at least an hour out." Kim scoffed, "We're not seeing her tonight."

Aaliyah rounded the corner from the kitchen holding a small bowl of ice cream and a spoon.

"So now what?" she asked.

Kim turned to her.

"I don't know. Do you mind if we crash here for a while at least until we figure all this out? Both our houses are way too hot to be staying at alone."

"Y'all are welcome to stay but it's pretty hot here too," Aaliyah reminded her.

"Yeah, but I figure we'd all fare better together rather than alone right now."

"True," Aaliyah shrugged.

Kim turned back to Rin, "Text her and ask her if she can stop by in the morning before she goes to the gym. Tell her it's urgent."

Rin nodded and began typing away on her phone.

"You think we got the time to be waiting until tomorrow though?" Aaliyah asked.

"I don't know, I hope so. Rin and her are pretty close, I feel like if something happened she'd have told her for sure."

"We'll see I guess," Aaliyah said downing a spoonful of ice cream.

Kim looked back to Rin.

"You got a change of clothes I can borrow?" Kim asked.

"Yeah," she nodded, "unlock the car."

"Make yourselves at home," Aaliyah said behind a spoonful of ice cream, "help yourself to whatever you can find in the kitchen. I mean, I'm vegan now so I doubt you'll find much in there you like but still."

As Kim walked by her she curiously eyed the bowl she was holding. She looked up at Aaliyah and raised her eye brows.

"Vegan?" she asked, "Ice cream isn't…"

"Look, I've had a long week alright."

Kim rolled her eyes and chuckled to herself as she followed Rin outside.

~

The sound of the doorbell made Kim flinch and immediately open her eyes. She was sitting with her legs crossed in the middle of Aaliyah's living room floor. Over the last few years she had revisited meditation and it had become a regular occurrence in her daily morning routine. Over time becoming easier and more effective, it had gone from something she decided to try, to something she loved. However, with the past two days being as crazy as they had been she had neglected to do so. She needed it this morning, after a long, nearly sleepless night, to unwind and allow her mind to settle.

She looked over at the grandfather clock in the corner and read "9:07" on its face.

Aaliyah came out from the kitchen heading towards the front door. After a quick peek through the peephole she opened the door. Charlotte stood on the front porch with a hand on her hip. She looked better than she had four years prior, a product of working out of her gym every day. She and Aaliyah traded warm smiles.

"My girl, it's been a minute," Aaliyah cheesed at her.

"Way too long familia," Charlotte grinned back.

They both extended a hand and pulled each other in for a long embrace.

"Good to see you," Aaliyah whispered over her shoulder.

"You too," she echoed.

Kim stood to her feet looking over towards them. Charlotte caught eye of her and her smile grew wider.

"Hey stranger," she teased.

"Hey," Kim said managing a slight smile, "how you been?"

"Busy, workin, livin," she shrugged.

"Good," Kim said.

Some sort of comfort came over Kim being in the same room as both of them; it felt nostalgic. She was beyond happy to see them alive and smiling, yet felt awful for the circumstances under which they were meeting. They, like her, had moved on from the sinful past they all shared and found new, peaceful lives to live, though she feared they were all soon to be robbed of that peace.

Rin walked out of the kitchen with a glass of tea in each of her hands. She froze as she saw

Charlotte. Charlotte's smile immediately faded and she stared daggers at her.

"How long you playin hooky for huh? You showin up Monday or should I just start lookin for someone to replace you now?"

Rin rolled her eyes at her.

"I'm off today, I'm not obligated to talk to you about work right now," she said holding one of the glasses out to Kim.

Charlotte scoffed at her remark as Aaliyah laughed at their exchange.

"You hungry?" Aaliyah asked. "We got a little left over from what we cooked this morning."

"Nah, I'm good, and actually I can't stay too long anyway. I got some early pilates classes this morning so while this little reunion is nice and all, it's gonna have to be a short one cause I gotta run."

Aaliyah looked back to Kim and Rin. Kim set her glass on the table and stepped forward.

"Have you noticed anything weird lately? You being followed or anything like that?"

Charlotte looked surprised by her question.

"By who?" she asked.

"Anyone, any attacks or anything like that?"

"Attacks? No? Why?"

Kim twisted her lips and began to think.

"So," Aaliyah began, "long story short, Thursday someone broke in here and attacked me, and then Friday two guys attacked Kim at a grocery store, she ended up havin to kill them both to get away."

Charlotte's eyes grew wide and her focus immediately shifted to Kim.

"That was you on the news? I saw that."

"Yeah," Kim sighed, "and then yesterday some guy followed me from The Home to Rin's house."

"That's odd," she said.

"Well not really, because the guy who followed her home and the one who broke in here both had these on them," Aaliyah said holding out the voice recorders. Charlotte looked down at them confused.

"What are those?" she asked.

Aaliyah pressed play on the first one.

"Kim, if you're listening to this then that means everything that I believe to know about you is true. You don't know me, but I know you oh so well."

Even after a third time hearing it the voice still made Kim's skin crawl.

"Knew your parents even better, the ones who took you in that is. You know what this is, you know what this is about. And in time, you'll suffer for all of it."

Charlotte looked up towards Kim. Kim simply shrugged.

"Wh-what…" Charlotte stuttered.

"Hold up, one more," Aaliyah said pressing play on the other.

"Aaliyah, life has been so kind to you these past few years hasn't it? No job, no responsibilities, no obligations, free from what enslaved you for so long. But what got you here? Sin. A whole lotta sin. And you will answer for those sins, every single one."

50

Charlotte looked up towards Aaliyah who shrugged as well. "Who is that?"

"No clue, don't know what they want or what this is about...." Kim said.

Rin sucked her teeth at her, "We know what this is about, we at the very least know that, whether y'all wanna admit it or not."

The room went silent for a moment.

"Is it...." Charlotte began.

No one answered.

"Ummm.... do y'all have one mentioning me or..." she asked.

"No, that's why we wanted to talk to you. If this is what we think it is, which we *don't know yet*," Kim said directing her words towards Rin, "whoever's behind this is more than likely sending someone at you eventually."

"Right," Charlotte said thinking heavily, "I mean, I haven't seen anything or anyone funny, but then again I haven't really been looking either."

"Well, you might wanna start," Aaliyah suggested.

"Yeah, I'll keep y'all updated, thanks for the heads up. I gotta run but we can link up tonight after I close up, try to make some sense out of all this."

"We'll be here, me and Rin are stayin here until we figure somethin out."

"I'll drop by after work then."

Kim nodded.

"Well, hey all that aside for now, can we all agree to just stay in touch a little more?" Aaliyah asked, "We're family, we shouldn't be goin years without seeing or hearing from each other."

Kim suddenly remembered how easygoing Aaliyah always managed to be. Even in the face of something so unknown she managed to turn the moment lighthearted.

Charlotte laughed, "Tsk…. I got a new phone twice since we last talked, I don't even have your number anymore."

"See, you slippin," Aaliyah said.

Charlotte pulled out her cell phone and attempted to unlock it but it failed to turn on.

"Ugh, it's dead. Forgot to throw it on the charger when I got in last night. I'll get you in tonight."

"Cool, I'm headed out right behind you. Mom's guilt tripped me into church today, if I'm late my name'll be mud."

"Good, you could use some church," Charlotte teased.

"I know you ain't talkin, you're no more a saint than I am," Aaliyah clapped back.

Charlotte shrugged. She walked over to Kim and hugged her.

"Good to see you, chica."

"You too."

She headed for the door.

"I expect to see you Monday morning Rin!" she called over her shoulder.

"I'm off the clock, you're not my boss right now!" Rin called back.

Aaliyah shook her head smiling at them both. She grabbed her keys from a small hook on the wall.

"Do me a favor and finish cleaning up the kitchen. I'll be back around one-ish. Y'all both got my number, text me if you need anything," Aaliyah said heading out the door.

"Alright," Kim said.

The door closed and Kim collapsed down into the sofa behind her. She let out a deep sigh and stared at the ceiling. She began tracing the letters of her name on her chain's charm. As she looked up, she saw Rin creep into her line of sight. She was looking down shooting her an uneasy stare.

"Please, don't say anything, just let me suffer in silence for a little bit," Kim pleaded.

Rin rolled her eyes. "Fine," she extended her hand out, "come help me with the kitchen."

Kim grabbed her hand and Rin pulled her to her feet. She ground her teeth together in frustration as she followed her into the kitchen.

"I got the dishes, you can clear off the table and take the trash out," Rin said turning on the water.

"Alright."

"You still goin to see Cindy tomorrow?"

"Supposed to but…. I don't know now. I don't want anyone following me up there putting her or anyone else in danger," Kim said raking food into the garbage.

"You said you don't think they're trying to harm innocents though."

"Yeah, *I don't think*, but I've been wrong before."

Rin shrugged. "Have you mentioned anything to her?"

"No, when I told her I was done with the assassin stuff she was beyond relieved. She'd never admit it but she hated me doin that mess, it scared her, she just hid it behind a bunch of jokes."

Rin turned off the water and looked over her shoulder with a devious smile.

"So are you finally admitting this has something to do with all that?"

Kim cut her eyes at her. Rin shrugged. Kim was about to rebuttal when she saw something black quickly move past the window behind Rin. Kim's eyes grew wide and her mouth fell open a bit. Rin immediately noticed her change of expression.

"What?" she asked.

Kim quickly walked over and shoved her out the way. She looked left and right out the window but saw nothing.

"What's wrong?" Rin asked.

"I saw something…." Kim said.

Rin peeked over her shoulder looking out the window as well.

"What?"

"I don't know but…"

Suddenly the doorbell rang drawing both their attention away from the window. They looked at each other, they were both completely still.

"She didn't say anyone was coming by did she?" Kim asked in a whisper.

"Maybe it's her? Maybe she forgot something?" Rin suggested.

"She has her keys, she wouldn't ring the doorbell to her own house."

Kim nodded in the direction of the door. Rin began to slowly make her way to it but before she could the sound of glass shattering upstairs halted her. She looked up, and turned back towards Kim. Kim looked up as well, listening, waiting. Suddenly the doorbell rang again. Rin continued looking at Kim waiting for her word.

"Call Aaliyah," Kim said.

Suddenly a figure in black crashed through the window behind Kim putting her in a headlock. She struggled, tugging at the muscular arms wrapped around her neck. Unable to move she lowered her chin and bit down hard on the attacker's bicep. They let out a deep wince that sounded like it belonged to a man. His grip around her neck loosened and she flipped him over her back onto the floor. She then tried to stomp him but her foot was caught, twisted, and she was flipped onto the floor.

Rin attempted to make a move towards them but froze as she heard footsteps coming down the stairs. She looked to her left just as three throwing blades passed right in front of her. Two of them stuck into the kitchen table while one hit the edge and fell to the floor. Rin quickly dropped and slid behind the wall leading into the living room. She pressed her back to the wall and frantically looked around. She saw the blade that had hit the floor just in her reach. She grabbed and held it tightly in her fist. Before she could settle another figure dressed in black stepped out from the kitchen and stabbed at her head with a knife. She ducked it, and stabbed the leg of the attacker with the blade she had picked up. She too heard a man's voice groan from behind the mask he was wearing. She quickly stood, grabbed his arm and twisted it. She then spun around and pulled the man over her shoulder flipping him onto the coffee table in the middle of the living room. The glass shattered as he crashed down onto it. She grabbed his hand still wielding the knife and forced it into his neck.

In the kitchen Kim rose to her feet with the man she had flipped over her back. He rushed forward trying to grab her but she knocked his hands away and pressed her own into his chest shoving him away. As he stumbled backwards she delivered a quick elbow to his face, grabbed a plate from off the table behind her, and smashed it over his head. He fell back into the counter a bit dazed.

Rin rushed back into the kitchen just as the front door was kicked in. She turned and saw another man in black enter. Before she could move the window just to her right shattered and another man came crashing through it. He swung his fist at her but she blocked the strike and shoved him back into the wall. She was then grabbed from behind by the other who had kicked down the door. He bent her left arm back restraining her as the other grabbed her right. She struggled to break free but couldn't.

Kim quickly looked to her right at a small pot sitting on the stove. She grabbed it, struck the man leaning against the counter with it in the head, and then hurled it at the ankle of the man holding Rin's arm behind her. He released her grabbing at his ankle and dropped to a knee. With one arm now free Rin poked the man still holding her in his eyes and slammed his head back into the wall behind them. He released her arm grabbing at his head. She then grabbed a steak knife resting on the table and stuck it into his stomach. He began slowly sliding down the wall.

The man who had first attacked Kim grabbed her from behind by her shoulders and spun her around to face him. She again began struggling to break free from his grasp. He eventually overpowered her and lifted her up off her feet. He tossed her away and she landed on the kitchen table sliding backwards. She quickly looked to both her left and right. While still on her back she grabbed a steak knife from her right and threw it at him. She looked to her left and grabbed the two throwing blades that had stuck into the table and threw them as well. The man managed to knock the first two away with swipes of his arm but the third hit him in his neck. He immediately dropped to the floor.

Kim looked left and saw the man she had thrown the pot at back on his feet rushing towards her with a blade in his hand. As he ran past, Rin swiped at his arm with the knife she had picked up. She cut through his sleeve and he lost his stride taking his focus off Kim to look at the gash on his arm. Kim pushed herself up to a crouching position on the tabletop. She grabbed the man by his arm, pulled him in close, and punched him in his gut. She grabbed his wrist, forced the knife he was holding into his stomach, and slammed his head down on the edge of the table. Knocked out he began to fall backwards. Kim stood up on the table and placed her foot on the man's chest. As he fell back, she leaned forward and used his body as a step to break her fall to the floor.

She looked around carefully, the house was quiet. She looked at Rin and they silently assured each other they were OK. Kim walked out of the kitchen to where the front door once stood. She poked her head outside looking up and down the street. She saw nothing, she really wasn't quite sure what she was even looking for.

"Uhhh…. Kim?" Rin called from the kitchen.

She took one last quick scan of outside before pulling her head back in. She rejoined Rin in the kitchen to find her crouched over the body of one of the men. She stood holding another voice recorder in her hand. She pressed play.

"You did it Charlotte, you beat the odds." the voice chuckled, *"You went from a stone-cold killer, an inhabitant of this hellhole of a city doin just as much dirt as anyone else…. hmph…. probably more really…. to a successful business owner. You should be proud. Proud you escaped with your life, proud you found something honest to sustain yourself, there were so many before you that weren't so fortunate. But I wonder, what would you be without that business, without that sustenance? Let's find out."*

The recording ended and Kim and Rin's eyes met. They shared fear-stricken expressions.

"Call Charlotte," Kim said.

Rin reached in her pocket for her phone but froze before pulling it out. A look of worry came over her. She looked like she had seen a ghost.

"Her phone was dead," Rin reminded her.

Kim quickly grew even more shaken.

"We gotta go!" she gasped.

~

Kim and Rin's jaws dropped as they arrived on the street Charlotte's gym was on. They both gazed at the building in awe seeing it engulfed in flames. Kim parked her car on the opposite side of the street. She and Rin jumped out and weaved their way in between the bumper-to-bumper traffic. As they got closer to the building they heard the panicked chatter of the few dozen watching the blaze from the parking lot.

"Oh god, Charlotte," Rin said spotting her.

She was sitting on the asphalt with her back up against her car with her hands over her mouth. She was being held by Hannah. Kim and Rin rushed over. Rin knelt down next to her and placed a hand on her shoulder.

"Hannah what happened?" Rin asked in a panic.

"A bunch of people in masks just ran in and started tossing molotovs or something inside, we couldn't put the fires out fast enough, they swallowed everything up whole," she said with tears in her eyes.

Kim's heart sank as she watched Charlotte bawl uncontrollably. She knew how hard she had worked, how much she had put into the gym to get it up and running, and to see it all going up in flames broke her.

Suddenly a man and woman burst out from the main entrance of the building. Clouds of black smoke spewed out from the doors behind them. The woman appeared to be crying fighting back against the man as he dragged her out of the building. Kim, looking at his shirt, immediately noticed the man was a staff member of the gym.

"Stop! Let me go, my daughter's still in there!" the woman wailed.

Kim's heart dropped. Everyone watching the fire from afar gasped hearing her panicked cries.

"Ma'am, I'm sorry, I can't let you go back in there!" the man said as he pulled her along.

Kim looked down to where Rin, Charlotte, and Hannah sat.

"There's still people inside?!" she asked.

Hannah shrugged. Kim immediately ran forward towards the building. Rin quickly stood and chased after her. Kim stopped as she came up to the man and woman still fighting each other.

"Is there someone still in there?" Kim asked them.

"My daughter!" the woman screamed with tears running down her cheeks, "My daughter was in the children's area!"

"Ma'am, we have to get away from the building. You too," the man said reaching out to grab Kim's arm.

Kim pulled back away from him and shot him a nasty look.

"Not while there's a kid in there, someone's gotta go get her!" Kim insisted.

"We called the fire department and they're on their…"

"The fire department?! What?! We don't have time to wait on the Joy City fire department!"

"Ma'am, please, I really need you to get back," he pleaded.

Kim snatched a small towel the man had resting over his shoulder and ran past him up to the gym's main entrance. She placed a hand on the door handle but stopped feeling a tug on her arm. She looked back and saw Rin.

"What are you doing?!" Rin asked.

"There's a little girl still inside! Where's the kid's area?!" she asked.

"Straight to the left," Rin said.

"Stay out here, hold the door open, I'll be right out," she told her.

She tucked her chain into her shirt, placed the towel over her mouth and nose, yanked the door open, and stepped inside. Even behind the towel she gagged, still able to taste and smell the smoke surrounding her. She crouched down trying to stay beneath the smoggy clouds and began taking small steps to the left. While she couldn't see them she could tell from the amount of smoke and how stuffy the air was the fires inside were large.

She eventually came to the tall wooden door and saw it was completely on fire. The bottom of the door was nearly just a pile of ashes resting on the floor while the upper portion was falling apart as it burned. She knelt down right in front of what was left of the burning door.

"Hey?! Hey anyone in there?!" Kim called.

"Yes! Yes, hello?!" a woman's voice called back.

"Are you OK, is it just you in there?!" Kim asked through a series of nasty coughs and dry heaves.

"No, there's a child in here with me, we can't get out!"

"Get away from the door I'm comin in, stay low beneath the smoke!"

Kim stood up and kicked hard at the bottom of the door. A large burning chunk of it fell to the ground. She kicked several more times stopping only to stomp her foot on the ground to extinguish small flames on the bottom of her shoe. Once she had kicked off enough of the bottom half of the door, she crawled over the smoldering pile of wood and into the room.

Once she had cleared the door she looked up and saw a petite blonde woman wearing a staff shirt sitting in the corner of the room. Wrapped tightly in her arms with her head covered in a blanket was a little girl crying into her chest. Kim crawled over to them and noticed the woman's leg had been badly burned.

"Are you alright?!" Kim asked.

"I can't walk, I tried to slide under the door with her but it was too low," she cried.

Kim looked back towards the door and saw that the wood she kicked off from the door had ignited and spawned a flame they wouldn't be able to get back over.

She looked around the room and saw the tall glass window leading outside. There was a large poster covering the entire window so that it couldn't be looked through from the inside or out.

"Hand me her," Kim said, "we gotta go through the window! Once I get her outside I'll come back and carry you out alright?!"

They traded, Kim gave her the towel to cover her face and the woman handed the child over to her. Kim took the blanket as well throwing it over the child's head. She quickly walked over to the window and tore the poster down. Daylight flooded into the dark clouded room.

Kim took a deep breath and struck the glass hard with her elbow breaking a small hole in it. Her inhale sent her into a coughing fit as smoke entered both her mouth and nose. She coughed so hard she became light headed and dizzy. She braced against the cracked window for a second to gather herself. She took another deep breath, stood, and began delivering several more strikes to the window until there was a big enough hole for the little girl to be passed through. Rin immediately appeared on the other side.

"Is the kid OK?!" she asked.

"Yeah, I got her here!" Kim gagged passing the little girl to her.

Rin grabbed her and carefully set her on the ground.

"There's someone else in here!" Kim gasped.

"Another kid?!"

"No, a worker! Make the hole bigger, she's injured I'm gonna have to carry her out!"

Kim and Rin started pulling pieces of jagged glass away to widen the hole enough for Kim to step through it. Once they got it large enough Kim stepped back and viewed the hole. It was low, she would have to duck but she didn't feel they had the time to do any better.

"Alright alright, good enough!" Kim said, "Back up I'm gonna grab her!"

Kim turned around and her entire body went stiff. Standing in front of her was not the woman she had found holding the child but someone standing just slightly shorter than herself. Wearing an oversized sleeveless top and a pair of jean shorts that came only a few inches down her legs. Kim's racing heart suddenly stopped as she looked up from the person's attire to their face and saw a smile. A smile she hadn't seen in four years. She went completely numb.

"Miss me?" Helena cheesed in her face.

Kim quickly looked her up and down unable to speak, she couldn't believe it.

"Kim! Kim, what's wrong?!" Rin called from behind her.

Remembering she was standing inside a burning building Kim shoved Helena aside and stumbled over to the woman. She picked her up and walked her over to the busted window. She turned sideways with the woman in her arms and eased out the building.

Covered in soot, gasping for air Kim walked the woman over to the hood of a car and placed her on top of it. Rin immediately started to treat the woman's wound.

Kim turned around to be emphatically thanked and embraced by the child's mother. Kim, so out of breath, couldn't even utter a response back. She simply nodded in return and pushed the woman aside. She stumbled over to a concrete wall separating the gym's parking lot from the one beside it and collapsed onto her hands and knees. She spat on the asphalt a few times trying to remove the horrid taste of smoke and ash from her mouth.

She turned over and pressed her back to the wall looking back towards the building. The blaze had grown wilder. She sat in a complete loss for words. She had thought the days of her life consisting of events as such had long passed, but there she sat.

What is happening she asked herself.

"It's sad really, she worked so hard to build the place, and to lose it like this…."

Kim looked up and to her right and saw Helena sitting on the concrete wall. She thought she had to be dreaming at first but it was really her. Blonde hair, green eyes, the rose tattooed on her shoulder, the feather hanging from the string around her neck. She was in the exact same clothes she had seen her in four years ago when she first bumped into her at the grocery store. She even had on the black beanie she left on Kim's doorstep. She didn't look like she had aged a day.

"H-Helena?" Kim asked.

65

Helena looked down at her and smiled big. Kim knew then it had to be her, there was no one else that had a smile like hers.

"C'mon K, who else you know that's this fine?" she laughed.

Kim's head was pounding. She thought it was due to how hard she had been coughing from the smoke and heat inside the building but was now believing otherwise.

"W-why, why are you here?" Kim asked puzzled.

Helena's smile faded and she offered Kim a look of curiosity in response to her question. She seemed surprised by her asking.

"Good question Kim," she looked deep into her eyes and smugly smiled, "why am I?"

~

Kim turned off the water and stepped out of the shower onto a cold tiled floor. She looked back and frowned at the black soot filled water slowly spiraling down the drain. She dried herself off and carefully rewrapped her arm. The cut stung from a bit of soap that had gotten into it while she was bathing. She threw on a lime green shirt and a pair of leggings that belonged to Rin. She looked in the mirror and saw the shirt was one of her work shirts. Across the front in bold white letters it read, "Wellness Pool."

Kim bit her lip and released a heavy sigh. Confusion, fear, disappointment, anger, and many other emotions fought for dominance inside her mind. She wasn't sure which one was more dangerous to submit to at the moment.

She wrapped her clothes in the towel she had dried off with and left out the bathroom. She walked to the left down a short hallway into an open living room; a living room she remembered sleeping in many nights as a teenager when she would run away from The Home. As she entered four pairs of eyes fell on her; Rin's, Aaliyah's, Charlotte's, and Terrance's.

Terrance's age was immediately visible. He had grown his hair out to a low afro which had gone mostly grey along with his facial hair. The skin on his face looked a bit looser around his mouth and eyes, and he seemed to have lost a little weight. He still looked healthy, he was still recognizable, but it was obvious he hadn't been doing the same things he had four years prior. Living off the fortune he had accumulated and the many investments he made, he'd lived the last four years as his elderly parents' caretaker.

"Well?" Kim asked.

Terrance shook his head as he placed one of the voice recorders down on the coffee table next to the two others.

"Judging from those, sounds like y'all are right, you're bein hunted," he said.

His voice was deeper than she had remembered it.

"But by who?" she asked.

Terrance shrugged, "I don't recognize the voice, but he knows y'all by name and knows too much of your business, *our* business."

Kim found it amusing that even Terrance, the orchestrater of it all, dared not speak the name. Even to him it was taboo.

"OK, if this is about four years ago, then what?" Charlotte asked, her eyes red from crying, "Does anyone know someone who'd have a vendetta against us?"

"That list could go on forever," Aaliyah said.

"And they could be connected to anything or anyone that was in Joy City over the last decade, that'd be a witch hunt," Terrance added.

"So, then what, what are we supposed to do?" Aaliyah asked.

"I would say just lay low."

"Lay low?" Charlotte cried, "This guy's sending people to kill us?"

"I know but what else can you do right now, you don't have a lead to go on, the guy on this recording might as well be a ghost," Terrance said.

"I don't think he's sending those people to kill us," Kim said.

Everyone's attention immediately turned towards her. Kim looked to Rin.

"Earlier at the house, did it feel to you like those men were trying to kill us?" Kim asked.

Rin shot her a confused stare back. "Uhhh…. yeah? I'd say the knives they were throwing at us qualified as that."

"No. I mean, yes, they were trying to hurt us, but I don't think they're meant to kill us. The voice on the recordings said that we'd suffer for our sins. I don't think these are necessarily hits, they just want our attention."

The room fell quiet as they all begin to think.

"OK, even if that's true, so what? What does that mean?" Rin asked.

"I don't know yet, I haven't gotten that far," Kim admitted turning away from them.

"So, in the meantime we're all just supposed to stay looking over our shoulders every second making sure no one's on our tails?" Aaliyah asked.

"I'm sorry," Terrance shrugged, "at the moment I don't think y'all have much of a choice."

Aaliyah fell back into the couch shaking her head, "This is wild man."

"What about you?" Kim asked, "If he came for us there's no reason to think he wouldn't be coming for you too, eventually."

"And if he does, I'll be ready," he said.

His overconfidence in his ability to defend himself scared her a bit. He wasn't taking the matter as serious as she believed he should have been. He was much older and even further removed from actively killing than she was.

"We probably shouldn't stay here too much longer." Aaliyah said, "We're for sure someone's targets right now and maybe, just maybe, for some reason you're not seeing as how you haven't been attacked yet. But it seems like anywhere we go has the potential to be swarmed at any moment. Don't wanna bring that to your home, especially with your folks here."

"So where are y'all gonna go?" he asked.

They all looked back and forth amongst each other waiting for someone to speak up.

"Right now none of our houses are safe, we'll just have to figure something out. But yeah, we should probably get goin," Kim agreed.

"Alright well, be careful, keep me posted. Y'all know where to find me if you need me," Terrance said standing to his feet, "Y'all hungry? I can wrap y'all up something before you take off."

"Starving," Rin said standing.

"Me too," Aaliyah said rising as well.

Charlotte silently stood along with them.

"I'm good," Kim said, "I'm gonna step outside and get some air. Don't be long, we need to get away from here as soon as we can."

As the three of them followed Terrance into the kitchen Kim stepped out the front door onto the porch. The sun had set; the warm air had turned cool. She dropped the towel she had her clothes wrapped in and sat down on the porch's concrete steps. Her head hung low in defeat. Could her past truly still be haunting her, she wondered. Was there really no escape? She needed answers, clarity from a sound mind, a mind she trusted: her own.

"I know you're here, my head's killing me. I need to ask you some things," she said aloud.

She heard a light chuckle come from behind her.

"Ask and you shall receive," Helena said sitting down beside her.

Kim made eye contact with her. It felt surreal, like seeing someone back from beyond their grave.

"Kim!" Helena joyfully cried, "I missed you, how you been babe?!"

Kim didn't answer her. She just continued staring at her blankly.

"Well, you look good, few crow's feet here and there but nothing a little cream can't take care of," Helena said poking Kim's cheek.

Kim quickly knocked her hand away and frowned.

"Why are you here?" Kim asked.

Helena sighed and crossed her arms. She seemed reluctant to answer.

"Kim, I haven't changed and neither has our connection to each other. I'm still your offset, and there's only one reason I'm ever on the outside of your brain."

Kim turned away from her and buried her face in her hands. She knew what she meant; she didn't have to say it.

"You asked for a sign the other night didn't you?" she smiled.

Kim cursed herself silently.

"Look," Helena shrugged, "I don't know what part of today it was, but somewhere during it all you snapped and didn't even know it."

"The kid," Kim said lifting her head, "that's where I draw the line, putting kids in danger."

"Maybe, might also have something to do with the fact that you're killing people again."

"I'm not, I was defending myself," Kim corrected her.

"OK, *defending yourself*," she rolled her eyes, "fine, fact is you're not well right now, mentally, I mean."

"I feel fine," Kim insisted.

"Ehhh, you feel a lot over a span of twenty-four hours, doesn't mean you're fine. Life's been pretty lax for you these last few years, your definition of what's fine and what's not has probably changed a lot. You may not feel like you felt when I first showed up years ago, not as much may be happening now as was then, but your brain is perceiving that something's wrong again, and so, here I am."

Kim instantly remembered how brilliant Helena could seem at times. How well she was able to explain and break things down.

"What do you know right now, did you watch the last four years of my life?" Kim asked.

"Did I watch them, no. Do I know them, yes. Why? I don't know. That's just how I seem to work."

Her uncertainty was alarming. Kim then remembered her confession four years ago that she didn't truly know everything about their connection.

"Do you know what's happening right now? Do you know why we're being hunted?" she asked.

"Still not psychic Kim," she smiled.

"Unbelievable…." Kim murmured.

"My advice, lie low like Terrance said, at least for now."

"I don't think there's any lying low right now, someone's on us, whether they want something from us or just want us dead we don't know, but they don't seem to be having much trouble finding us."

"Yeah, those recordings are uhhh.... pretty creepy, guy talks like an old evil snake. All y'all can do is just watch each other's backs at the moment, you know too little to do anything else."

Kim buried her face in between her knees.

"Hey, cheer up, least you're not alone," Helena threw her arm around her, "you got me."

Kim clinched her teeth as the pain in her head grew sharper.

Chapter 3

Kim III

Kim sat nearly motionless, slowly breathing in and out of her mouth. She kept her eyes closed, as her chest inflated and then fell back. Meditation had done wonders for her in recent years. The ability to mute the noise surrounding her and cease arbitrary thoughts from entering her mind had become effortless, but today she just couldn't. Her focus was shot.

She was sitting outside watching the younger kids of The Home as they darted all over the playground, or so she was supposed to be. The sound of the glass door sliding open behind her immediately forced her eyes open. She looked back over her shoulder and saw LuLu hanging out the door.

"Hey," she smiled.

"Hey, you just getting here?" Kim asked.

"Yeah," LuLu rolled her eyes, "stopped by the bank, everyone in Joy City had to be there this morning of course." She stepped outside, pulled one of the white plastic chairs up next to Kim, and took a seat.

"You still goin to see Cindy today?" LuLu asked.

"Yeah, I'mma bring the kids back inside in a few minutes and then take off. I just stopped by to help get them started this morning."

"She doin alright?"

"Yeah, she's got her last final today."

"Ugh…. finals," LuLu groaned, "I remember those."

"Fun times?" Kim teased.

"Tsk…. never," LuLu scoffed, "I remember one time…"

LuLu stopped and they both looked over their shoulders as the door behind them slid open again. Ms. C poked her head out.

"Ten more…. oh LuLu, did you just get here?" she asked.

"Yeah, I'm sorry, I would've been here sooner but I got held up at the bank."

"Oh it's fine, don't worry about it sweetheart. The city went kinda crazy yesterday with the fire and everything," she said.

"What fire?" LuLu asked.

"Downtown, that big gym that opened up a few years ago. I forget what it was called, but the building caught fire somehow yesterday and burned up."

"Downtown?" LuLu thought to herself for a second, "Wait, Wellness Pool?"

"Yep, that's it," Ms. C nodded.

LuLu immediately turned to Kim in shock.

"Doesn't your friend own that place?" she asked.

"Yeah…. I mean, she *did* anyway."

"Wasn't Rin working there too?" she asked.

"She *was*," Kim nodded.

"Oh my god," Ms. C stepped outside, "is she OK?"

"Yeah, she's fine, she wasn't even there when it happened. From what I heard no one got hurt."

"That's still terrible though. She built that place from the ground up," LuLu said.

"Yeah, I talked to her last night, she was pretty torn up about it."

"They don't know what caused it to catch fire?" Ms. C asked.

"From what she told me it didn't just catch fire, it was set on fire, they don't know by who or why though."

"Oh my goodness," Ms. C gasped.

Kim had been reliving parts of the previous three days all morning. She tried to connect whatever she could in hopes of uncovering some kind of lead, but to no avail. All she had were the vague warnings from the chilling voice in the recordings.

You don't know me, but I know you oh so well. Knew your parents even better, the ones who took you in that is.

…. in time, you'll suffer for all of it.

The messages spun in her head endlessly. She found it impossible not to wonder, yet she had no idea of where to even begin.

"Is she gonna rebuild it?" LuLu asked.

"She's not sure at the moment." Kim shrugged, "For right now I think she just wants to relax, let things calm down before she even thinks about doing anything."

"Yeah, that makes sense," LuLu said.

Kim stood and looked to Ms. C.

"Hey, I was gonna drive up to Cindy's school today to see her, are you guys OK here?"

"Oh yeah we'll be fine. We got plenty of help showin up today, go ahead." She turned to LuLu. "In about ten minutes bring them in OK?"

LuLu nodded.

"I'll see you later Lu," Kim said.

"Alright, tell Cin I said hey. Drive safe."

"I will," Kim said following Ms. C back inside.

They both walked through the building and then outside to Kim's car. Once outside Kim quickly scanned around making sure they weren't being watched by anyone.

"So, you knew the girl who owned the gym huh?" Ms. C asked.

"Yeah, she was a…. friend from school," Kim edged out.

Ms. C shook her head in disappointment. She looked up at Kim with twisted lips and shrugged.

"Joy City," she sighed.

"Yep, Joy City," Kim repeated.

Ms. C's slight frown slowly turned to a discreet smile.

"Well, drive safe. Tell Cindy I said hello, and that when she gets back out here she better come see me."

Kim smiled back at her, "I will."
They shared a hug and Kim drove off.

~

"Yesterday around ten o'clock the local gym, Wellness Pool, was set ablaze. Thankfully no one was critically injured in the fire but the damage to the building will unfortunately close the gym until further notice, much to the dismay of the many..."

"Ugh...." Helena reached for the knob and turned the radio's volume all the way down, "enough of that, tired of all this depressing talk."

Kim cringed over the report and a splitting headache she was suffering from as she drove. "Please don't touch my radio," she said.

Helena looked at her with a sideways smirk. She had her feet kicked up on the dashboard, her hands behind her head, and her seat reclined all the way back.

"Just as pleasant as always K," she sighed, "good to see you haven't changed."

Kim was still a bit uneasy seeing Helena again. Essentially it meant her mental state was so bad she was again suffering from hallucinations. Helena leaned forward in her seat and begin staring hard at Kim.

Kim glanced over at her for a quick second cutting her eyes at her, "What?" she asked.

"Nothin, just kinda insulted how you're sittin here actin like you didn't miss me." Helena's sarcasm was apparent by the huge grin on her face as she spoke.

"What are you talkin about?" Kim murmured.

" 'Helena, will I forget you when you disappear?' " Helena whined. She mocked Kim with an exaggerated tone and wide eyes that she batted repeatedly.

"Oh my god...." Kim breathed rolling her eyes.

" 'Are you ever gonna come back?' " Helena continued. She leaned over the center console and pressed her shoulder up against Kim.

"Can you stop?" Kim mumbled.

" 'Thank you Helena, for everything. I love you,' " she whimpered pretending to cry.

"Move!" Kim cried shoving her away.

Helena chuckled to herself. "I doubt you even shed a tear for me after that night. If you had it'd probably have come out a diamond or somethin."

Kim wondered what all she knew. The truth was while no, she never shed a tear for Helena, for the first couple of months after she disappeared Kim thought about her often. Late at night she would come downstairs for tea and find herself a bit disappointed at Helena's absence.

"Where were you all this time? Were you really just in my head?"

Helena reclined back into her seat.

"I think so."

"You think?"

"Remember when I said I didn't know everything about our connection, where I was or what

I was before we met? Well, that was true and I still don't. But I know enough and I know what's been happening out here since I disappeared."

"How much?"

"Enough," Helena shrugged.

Kim was then reminded of how Helena loved to be vague in answering questions. It was still as annoying as ever.

"I know you started volunteering at Little Angels shortly after that mess four years ago."

"Yeah…."

"Well, first off, I'm proud of you, K, that's huge."

Kim shrugged.

"Let's see," Helena put her fist under her chin as she began thinking, "LuLu graduated, Blake's a father, Ms. C is still the only person in Joy City with a clean conscience, Cindy finished high school and went off to college…."

Kim looked at her puzzled.

"How do you know all that?"

"Because you know it, we're the same brain remember? C'mon, it's only been four years, keep up," she cheesed.

It had been so long since she had seen her Kim had forgotten Helena wasn't her own person but an extension of herself.

"And speakin of everyone else's affairs, where's your man, where's your first born? I wouldn't mind another little niece or nephew," Helena poked.

"I don't have the patience for either."

Helena sucked her teeth at her response.

"C'mon K, you're pushin thirty, how'd you live the last four years all by yourself? You gonna live the rest of your life like that?"

"If I choose to it's none of your business anyway," Kim snapped.

"Just as delightful as I remember." Helena laughed. "At least tell me this Kim, have you been happy?"

Her question made Kim stop and think for a moment. She remembered Helena telling her once she already knew the answer to every question she asked her.

"Been happy?" Kim repeated.

"Take your time we got the ride there and back," Helena said looking out the window.

Kim only had to take a moment to consider. The obvious answer was yes. The years since she had last seen or spoken to Helena had been peaceful and relatively stress free. She honestly didn't have a complaint to speak of.

"Yeah, I've been happy.... but..."

"But what?"

"You're here, and something's telling me that means happiness may be coming to an end soon, if it's not already over."

Kim peeked at Helena out the corner of her eye and noticed the smile on her face soften for a moment.

"We'll get to that," she said, "first talk to me about bein happy."

"What about it?" Kim asked.

"The past four years have been good to you, what made them good?"

"I mean a lot happened I guess. With all the extra time, I ended up volunteering at The Home, that's been an amazing experience. Making a difference in kids' lives has changed my outlook on a lot, especially how I came up when I was in there."

"Makes a little more sense why Blake was always beggin you to come back now huh?"

"Yeah actually."

"Good, what else?"

"I guess I also had a lot more time to spend with Cindy. Me and her were able to grow a lot closer before she went off to school, that was a good thing."

"That was a *great* thing, you both needed and deserved that time together."

"Yeah…. I guess time and the freedom to do what I wanted with that time was what was so good. Time at The Home, time with Cindy, Lu, and of course Rin."

"Rin," Helena laughed, "yeah, talk to me about her, she's grown up a lot in the past four years huh?"

"I mean, she's practically not even the same person she was four years ago when we met. The two years she lived with me was basically a time of us just figuring out who we were. Neither of us had anything weighing us down anymore. I think that was the first time for either of us in our adult lives where we were able to just live. But who she is today is definitely not who she was Christmas four years ago, but like in a good way. I think Joy City toughened her up, made her a lot less naïve, a lot sharper."

"That's good. I remember when she touched down in Joy City she caused a lot of havoc," Helena giggled.

"Yeah, but she's learned a lot since. She was desperate then, she wasn't thinking clearly. She's actually incredibly smart, very intuitive, and having her around has been a huge blessing."

"Awww Kim, you love your little sister," Helena teased.

"God you ruin everything," Kim shook her head.

"OK OK, last thing. Just tell me this and I'll leave you alone, where are you with your parents?"

Kim again had to stop and think a bit. Truthfully, aside from the mention of her foster parents in the recordings, she hadn't thought about either pair of her parents in a while.

"My parents…. uhhh…. I don't know. I haven't really thought about them like that in a while."

"That's good, that means you're healing," Helena told her.

"I mean, I miss them, all four of them, but I haven't been stuck thinking about them in a while. Kinda weird now that I think about it."

"Life's been too good to focus on the bad, that's a blessing not a curse. You haven't been stuck on them for a while and you shouldn't ever be. Enjoy your peace Kim, enjoy your life."

"But it feels like that peace might be comin to an end," Kim said.

Still facing the road in front of her she peeked back over to Helena and noticed her smile had completely faded. She closed her eyes, sighed, and bit her lip conjuring up her response. Kim remembered these rare moments of silence when talking with Helena. When her smile left and she had to take a few seconds to think about what she was going to say next. Something profound usually followed.

"Kim, I'll say this, whatever all this is, whatever's happening, you'll make it out on the other side of it, just like you have with everything else life has thrown at you."

Kim took a moment to consider her words but ultimately found them to be empty. "And what makes you so sure?" she asked.

Helena's smile came back as she turned from the window and looked directly at Kim.

"As long as we've known each other, how many times have I been wrong?"

Kim fell mute.

~

Kim walked down the main concourse looking left and right. She had made it to the campus of Cindy's school and was looking for her and her dormmate who were supposed to be sitting outside at one of the picnic tables. She was also keeping a lookout for anything or anyone suspicious. While she knew it was risky, she convinced herself to make the drive with the hopes she wouldn't draw any unwanted guests along with her.

It was a small school that technically was in the next city over from Joy City. When looking for schools Cindy specifically looked for colleges outside of Joy City. Joy City had three local community colleges but none of them were too highly regarded. Cindy having never really been outside of Joy City her entire life also felt she just needed to see somewhere else for once. Kim couldn't blame her but asked her to consider a school close enough so they would be able to visit each other often. She found a happy medium for them only about two and a half hours away.

Kim had already traveled up to the school to visit three times during the school year. Each time as she walked about the campus she couldn't help but stare in awe at the architecture and landscaping. It was all so neat and well taken care of. The zigzag pattern of the cut grass, the checkered orange and blue bricks on every building, the stone cut pillars lining the concourse. Even the air felt different than what she was used to. Aside from the one trip she took back to the East Coast to help Rin pack and get her things shipped out to Joy City, Kim realized she had rarely ever been outside of the city's limits herself.

It was a bit of a culture shock at first. People passing by spoke or smiled at her. People just seemed so much more friendly than she ever knew strangers could be. Living in Joy City her whole life had truly sheltered her.

"Hey K, you ever regret not goin to college?"

Kim looked to her right and saw Helena walking beside her. She too was eyeing all around the campus.

"No, not really," she said.

"Hmph.... you know, if I were real, I think I'd have liked to go to college. Somethin tells me I'd have liked it," she smiled.

"You have thoughts like that?" Kim asked.

"Like what?"

"I mean that sounds like a desire. As something or someone that doesn't exist I just wouldn't expect you to have an affection or desire for anything that exists beyond your being."

"I exist Kim, just not to everyone else." she laughed, "You have wants and desires right? Well, we're of the same mind so why wouldn't I have them too?"

Kim couldn't dispute what she was saying but she couldn't say it made sense to her either.

"I guess," she shrugged, "so then what are some of your desires?"

Helena looked at her with wide eyes, obviously intrigued by her question. "Well truthfully..." she began.

Before she could finish a voice calling to Kim cut her short. "Hey Mom!"

They both looked ahead slightly to the right of the concourse and saw Cindy waving her hand at them from a picnic table. Helena smirked and

86

shrugged, "Remind me, we'll talk about it. Tell Cindy Aunt Helena said hello," before disappearing amongst a crowd of people walking by.

Kim recalled back to how supernatural Helena's timing always seemed to be when it came to revealing information. While she loathed it, it was also incredibly interesting. At times it almost seemed as if she was manipulating time herself causing random interruptions to leave Kim stuck anxiously wondering for answers.

Kim crossed over the concourse and stepped onto the grass making her way to the table Cindy was sitting at along with another girl. As she approached them Cindy stood and hugged her. She had grown a bit taller over the years nearly eclipsing Kim. Her hair was braided into cornrows on the left side of her head with the right side hanging down free. Her hair was also no longer pink. Towards the end of her senior year of high school she decided to ditch the dyed color for her natural blonde.

"Hey kid," Kim said squeezing her tightly, "missed you."

"Missed you too," Cindy smiled.

"Hey Lei-Ling, how are you?" Kim asked turning to the other girl sitting at the table.

Lei-Ling was Cindy's dormmate. She was born in China but raised mostly in America, fluent in both English and Chinese. As Cindy told it she was a brilliant student, extremely kind, and very quickly became her best friend once the school year started. She had long jet-black hair that fell down her back and bangs that fell just above her eyes. As Kim pointed out the first time she met her, she had an adorable baby face.

"I'm good Ms. Kim," Lei-Ling smiled. She spoke in a light and friendly tone as she stood and hugged Kim as well.

Kim sat down next to Cindy. "So, how were finals?" Kim asked looking between the two of them.

"Between the tests and having to actually study for them definitely the worst two weeks of my life," Cindy moaned.

"That's cause you only studied for like four hours a day," Lei-Ling laughed.

"That's all I had time for, I still had to eat and sleep," Cindy said.

Kim shook her head laughing.

"Do you at least think you passed everything?" she asked.

"I guess we'll find out eventually," Cindy mumbled.

Kim rolled her eyes at her.

"How do you think you did?" Kim asked looking to Lei-Ling.

"All mine were pretty easy, I'm pretty sure I passed all of them."

"I'm telling you, the girl's an android, I haven't seen her get anything below a B the whole year," Cindy said.

"Well, maybe you should adopt some of her study habits then?" Kim suggested.

"I tried to tell her," Lei-Ling said, "I offered to tutor her too."

"I don't have the endurance to do anything school related with you, I need my seven hours of sleep every night," Cindy said.

Kim and Lei-Ling conceded with slight shrugs.

"Anyway, Ms. C and LuLu said to tell you hello," Kim said.

"I haven't talked to Ms. C in a while, how is she?"

"She's good, still giving The Home a thousand percent of her entire being."

"That woman's a saint. I'll give her a call tonight. How's Aunt Rin? I heard the gym she was working at burned down yesterday."

A lump formed in Kim's throat. She hadn't expected Cindy to know anything of the happening.

"Ummm…. yeah, it was really crazy, apparently someone just ran in there and lit the place up."

"Your friend owned that place, right?"

"Yeah…. she took it pretty hard. She put a lot into that place."

"Do they know who did it or why?" she asked.

Kim shook her head no.

Cindy shook her head in disappointment. "Joy City…" she sighed looking down.

Kim's eyes fell to the table as she shared her anguish.

"This Joy City place, is it really that bad?" Lei-Ling asked.

Both Kim and Cindy's eyes rose up to her.

89

"Let's just say it's not a place you'd wanna visit, that's why I left and came here," Cindy explained.

Lei-Ling turned and looked at Kim.

"You still live there right? You never tried to move? What kept you there for so long, what's keeping you there now?" she asked.

Kim and Cindy glanced quickly at each other. Kim knew part of the answer to her question but it was the part she wasn't able to tell her. The part she could tell, truthfully, she didn't have an answer for. So, she lied.

"Work. Just packing up and leaving wouldn't be as easy as it sounds."

"I see," Lei-Ling nodded.

Kim and Cindy made discreet eye contact. Kim could feel the judgment in her glance.

"But nobody was hurt and Aunt Rin's fine, she'll just have to find another job for the time being," Kim said.

"Yeah, I guess. I'm really not looking forward to goin back to that city over the summer," Cindy said.

"I know, I wouldn't either if I lived here for almost a year. Speaking of that, now that finals are done when are you comin home?"

"I don't know yet, I'mma help her get moved into her apartment for next year and then I'll be heading that way."

Kim looked over to Lei-Ling with mild concern.

"You're not gonna go home over the summer?" she asked.

"No ma'am, my parents are getting me an apartment off campus for next year and then they're actually gonna come here and stay with me for a bit over the summer."

"Oh alright, that's good. Looks like you just lost your roommate though kid," Kim said to Cindy.

"Well, it's two bedrooms and two baths so we talked and if splitting the rent is OK after my parents head back home, she could move in," Lei-Ling explained.

"Sounds like a plan to me," Kim nodded.

"We'll figure it out." Cindy said standing. "We were waiting on you to get here before we ate, you hungry?"

"Yep, starvin, take me anywhere there's food," Kim said.

~

Kim gently nudged Lei-Ling's arm. "Tell the truth, she's tough to live with huh?" Kim whispered behind a smile.

Lei-Ling smiled back and laughed. They were sitting in the common area of Cindy and Lei-Ling's dorm. They had had lunch and Kim was getting ready to head back to Joy City.

"No, not at all, we had a great time this year. I'd heard so many college roommate horror stories but I guess I got lucky, everything's been great."

Kim playfully scoffed at her response. "We must be talkin about a different Cindy. The one I lived with was…"

Kim hushed as Cindy rounded the corner from her room. She immediately saw the guilty look on Kim's face and assumed the worst.

"Whatever she told you, it's not true," Cindy said.

Kim and Lei-Ling both stood from the couch.

"Take care, sweetheart, tell your parents I said hello, and keep in touch with us over the summer alright?" Kim said hugging her.

"Yes, ma'am, I will."

"I'mma walk her down, I'll be right back," Cindy told her.

She nodded and fell back into the couch. Kim and Cindy left out the door and headed down the stairs and out to the parking lot. As they got to Kim's car she grabbed Cindy by her arm and pulled her in close to her, kissing the top of her head and hugging her tight.

"Me and everyone back home are proud of you, can't wait till you get back home. Let us know when you're gonna be headin our way OK?"

"Yeah, I will, love you."

"Love you too."

Kim got in her car and started the engine. She looked out the window and noticed Cindy hadn't moved. She was just standing there with a sad anxious look on her face. Kim rolled her window down and leaned out.

"What's wrong?" she asked.

"When Lei-Ling asked you why you stayed in Joy City…"

Kim knew the conversation about her answer to Lei-Ling's question was coming, though she thought she would have more time to prepare for it.

"Cin, you know I couldn't tell her…"

"No, I know you couldn't tell her about…. *everything*, but that was then. What's keeping you there now?"

Kim thought for a moment. She didn't want to lie to her but she didn't quite know what the truth was either. Any excuse she had was admissible and she knew it just as well as Cindy did.

"I don't know," Kim shrugged.

Cindy was obviously unsatisfied with her answer as she looked away biting her lip.

"Is it crazy to just not really be able to see myself anywhere else?" Kim asked, "Regardless of how I feel about it, it's home. I've been there forever. Little Angels is there, Aunt Lu is there, Aunt Rin is there, my parents are buried there, all of them…. where else would I go?"

"Anywhere else," Cindy suggested.

Kim could hear desperation in her voice.

"Cin, what's up?" Kim asked.

"Yesterday, when I heard about the fire, it got me thinking. I was gonna wait until I got home to talk to you about it but…. I really want you to leave Joy City, for good."

Something about this was shocking to Kim. She knew how much Cindy despised the city, she despised it just as much really, but the thought of leaving never sat right with her.

"Why?" Kim asked.

"That fire hit a little too close to home. Aunt Rin works there, the owner was one of your friends. Joy City is just too…. Joy City. I still see all the stuff that happens there on the news. I saw a few days ago some woman was attacked by two guys in a parking lot, she ended up stabbing and killing both of them."

Kim bit her bottom lip in shame.

"After living here for a year, I'd just rather not have to keep goin back to that city, and so I really want you to think about movin away, you and Aunt Rin. It doesn't have to be far, that way you can both still be close to your parents but just somewhere else."

She spoke softly but the words she spoke were strong and deliberate. It was obvious she had done a lot of thinking about the subject and was now pleading her case. Kim thought about the recent attacks she had been the target of and couldn't help but wonder had she not been in Joy City would they have still happened? Her heart and mind offered a pair of contradicting answers.

"There's nothing keeping you there anymore, Aunt Rin either, she can find another job somewhere else. So why stay?" Cindy added.

Kim couldn't argue with her, her points were sound. "OK," Kim nodded, "tell you what, your Aunt Rin moved across the country to be closer to us, so we can't just up and leave her. I'll talk to her tonight and see what she thinks. If she's willing to, we'll think about it OK?"

"OK," Cindy said leaning into the window to hug her once more, "drive safe, call me when you get home."

"I will baby."

Kim watched as Cindy crossed the parking lot and entered her hall. Once Cindy was out of her sight, Kim slumped down into her seat and sighed hard. She hated how she was feeling. She hated the guilt of keeping secrets from those she loved. She was falling slave to her own conscience again, she could feel it, it was eating her alive. She cursed herself as she pulled out of the parking lot.

~

Kim parked her car on the side of the road, unfastened her seatbelt, and relaxed back into the seat. Exhausted, she rolled her neck a few times, and stretched her spine in every which way. Her body had become stiff from the drive back to Joy City. She reached in her pocket and pulled out her cell phone.

"I'm walking up now," she typed out and hit send as she got out of her car.

The sun had set; the air outside had grown cold. Kim looked around herself in all directions ensuring she wasn't being followed or watched. She began to walk down the road's shoulder until she came to an adjacent street leading south. She passed by a green street sign that read "Comet" and turned. The road was dark and quiet. As she looked down the road she saw a dead end. Reaching it, she looked over her shoulder once more ensuring she was unseen before cutting into the woods that ended the road.

She found a narrow dirt path and followed it, stepping over and around the wild growing shrubs until the woods opened up to the old abandoned pool hall. It looked even worse than it had in its dilapidated state four years prior. The wooden boards that had been nailed over the windows had been stripped off and placed in a pile on the ground. A large blue tarp covered the front entrance, its lower half gently blowing from the calm night's breeze. Several strips of yellow police tape circled the small structure, most of which had been ripped through and now lay scattered about in the dirt. Kim felt a strange aura about the place as she stared at it; it felt like death.

She approached the pool hall stepping over garbage and tall green life in her path. She walked up the two wooden steps leading up the pool hall's wraparound porch towards the main entrance that had been tarped off, and stood there for a second. Standing in front of the pool hall's main entrance felt strange to her, she had never used it, no one had for decades.

She grabbed the tarp and pulled it aside. A horrid stench hit her nose; a mix of rotting wood, dust, and mold. She stepped inside and heard the sound of wooden floors creaking loudly from her slight movement. Immediately to her left was a medium sized room, the door to the room had been taken off the hinges. Inside there was nothing but four walls, yet she could remember a time not so long ago when there had been more; a desk, a few chairs, a filing cabinet or two. The right side of the doorframe and parts of the wall around it were riddled with bullet holes. She gnawed on her bottom lip as bitter memories of a friend and his sacrifice put a knot in her stomach.

She walked forward until she came to the main area of the pool hall. It was empty except for four sleeping bags placed in each corner of the room and a small lit kerosene lantern in the middle of the floor. The two billiards tables and folding chairs that always rested in the middle of the floor were gone and the two flat screen TVs had been ripped from the walls leaving holes with severed wires spilling out. As she scanned the room she noticed how much bigger it looked empty.

After the police raided the pool hall and were unable to find anything incriminating, they taped it off and demanded its electricity and water be cut. Anything that wasn't the floor, the walls, or the nails that kept the place standing was taken out to be investigated, leaving the inside of the hall looking just as barren as the outside.

The police's investigation of the pool hall and the things found inside it only lasted a few months. Rin's tip had essentially led them to a dead end, as the evidence needed to form a case had been reduced to ashes just before they arrived. The news reported Joy City officials talked of bulldozing the building, fearing whatever infractions it gave home to may start up again if they didn't level it. But crime in Joy

City never ceased. Even with the decline in the city's homicide rate due to The Pool's fall there was still too much for the Joy City Police Department to handle. There just wasn't enough of a reason to spend time and resources investigating something they had no actual evidence of. And so, the inside was cleaned out and the investigation was left cold. The pool hall was never knocked down.

With nowhere else to go, fearing their own homes were compromised and staying with anyone else could put innocents in danger, Kim, Rin, Aaliyah, and Charlotte crashed at the pool hall after leaving Terrance's house the night prior. It was the only place that was still nowhere on any map or radar, even after the events of four years ago.

Charlotte was asleep in her corner and Aaliyah was silently meditating in hers. As Kim entered the main area of the pool hall Rin lifted her head up from her sleeping bag.

"Hey, any issues today?" Kim asked.

"No. Quiet day for us, you?

"Same."

"How's Cindy?" she asked.

"She's good, she was..."

Charlotte slowly turned over in her sleeping bag and eyed both Rin and Kim through tired eyes. They both caught the hint. Rin stood, slipped on a black jacket lying near her sleeping bag, and eyed towards outside. They both quietly tip toed out.

"Let's go around back, we don't need to be out in the open," Kim said.

They rounded the building cutting further into the dense woods behind the pool hall. They fought their way through weeds, hanging branches, and thorny shrubbery until they came to a large open area that was mostly free of plant life. It looked like a large dirt pit but in the center was a small mass of water. The water was dirty with tall grass sticking up and patches of moss floating in it. Rin eyed the area curiously.

"What is this?" Rin asked.

Kim raised an eyebrow at her question. "You never seen a swamp before?" she asked.

Sitting in the dirt were two tree stumps. Kim sat down on one and motioned for Rin to sit on the other. Slowly she inched down almost as if she didn't trust it.

"As long as the pool hall has been here, so has this swamp, as far as I know anyway. The first couple months after I joined The Pool I couldn't hardly stomach what I was doing to people. Every time I'd complete a contract I'd end up throwing up right after. One time I managed to actually make it all the way back here before getting sick. I ran into the woods cause I didn't want Terrance to think I was soft or whatever and ended up here. After that I started to come back here sometimes and just sit for a bit, just to think. Something about it was peaceful to me, it was always still, always quiet and calm. At times it felt like one of the most beautiful places in Joy City. I actually haven't seen it in like eight or nine years, I'm surprised how much it hasn't changed."

"Peaceful huh? I can see it," Rin said.

They sat quiet for a moment. Both their eyes wandering about the swamp aimlessly as the chirping of crickets rattled in their ears.

"Hey," Kim began with a quivering lip, "I'm sorry for all this." She looked straight as she spoke. She seemed unable to look directly at Rin.

"I know you didn't sign up for all this when you agreed to stay out here. When I joined The Pool I had one fear. It wasn't dying, it wasn't getting caught, it was the thought of the people who chose to associate themselves with me being put in danger because of it. I swore to myself if I was gonna do it, I was gonna keep everyone I loved out of it, but I…"

"Hey, listen," Rin stopped her, "it's fine. Do you remember how we met? In an alley trying to kill each other on Christmas Eve. You think I expected a normal relationship after we started out like that? No, I'll admit I didn't expect to be sitting in a swamp on the run from a guy who has some kind of grudge against you and your friends, but it's where we are, what can we do about it?"

"But it's a grudge against me not you. You shouldn't have to…"

"Kim," Rin sucked her teeth, "I shouldn't have to do a lot of the things I do for you, but I do them, just like you do for me. When I blew up the thing that'd fed you, your friends, and your foster parents for years you could've disowned me as your sister, you could've killed me on the spot, but you didn't. This isn't ideal for any of us. I'm sure we'd all love to be sleeping in our own beds waking up tomorrow

100

without a care in the world, but that's just not the life we're living right now. Regardless of who we wanna point fingers at, we're all in it and that's just it. And you're my sister, my *twin* sister, any grudge against you is one against me too."

Rin had grown so much wiser in such a short amount of time, it amazed Kim sometimes.

"OK but, I still feel bad about loopin you into all this," Kim mumbled.

"And that's fine, you can feel bad about it all you want, but I'm here, I'm in this with you, and I'm not goin anywhere."

"Thanks," Kim said.

"So, how's my niece doin?" Rin asked.

"She's good, finished up her finals. I'm proud of her. Had my life not ended up so crazy I'd like to think I would've ended up in college myself, it's good to see her there and doing well."

"I knew she'd do well, kid has a good head on her shoulders."

"Sometimes," Kim laughed.

"Hey, give yourself credit, you did a good job with her."

"Yeah? I like to think I made a difference in her life, a positive one."

"What? C'mon, of course you did." Rin insisted, "If everyone in this town made an honest effort to make a positive change in someone's life the way you did when you adopted her this swamp might not be the most beautiful place in the city."

They shared a brief laugh.

"All it takes is effort really. I'm not the perfect parental figure for her, far from it, actually, but I try. That's what makes the difference, that's the change in itself."

"Taking in a whole kid though? I don't think I could do it."

"Not just adopting, I mean anything. You can make a change doing anything, but first you have to do something. One action could birth something that lasts forever. I think that's where a lot of people miss their callings in life, they never act on anything so they're never able to leave their mark on the world."

"I've always wanted to say I was able to make some kinda change in this world. Somethin that when I'm gone people would say, *yeah, she did that*. But one action creating something that lasts forever?" Rin shrugged, "I don't know, it'd have to be one big action."

"No, not necessarily."

"Then how?" Rin asked.

Kim scanned the dirt beneath their feet. She reached down and picked up a small silver colored rock and stood.

"Stand up," she told Rin.

"What?"

"Stand up," she repeated.

Rin stood. Kim held out the rock for her to take. Rin took the rock in her hand still staring at Kim confused.

"Take a good look at it," Kim said, "really get to know it."

Rin's stare turned from one of confusion to one of almost fear. Kim's odd instruction had her completely lost. "Get to know it?" she asked.

"Just look at it," Kim rolled her eyes, "feel it, get a good idea of how it feels in your hands, get a good mental picture in your head of how it looks. Hurry up, so we can get back inside, it's cold out here."

Rin began to fondle the small rock in her hands, running her thumbs and fingers over its rough and jagged exterior. She looked over it for a few seconds flipping it over several times in her hands until she had viewed it from every angle. She looked up at Kim with her eye's cut.

"Is there a point to this?" she asked.

"Yes, now, throw it in the water," Kim said.

"Just…. throw it?"

"Yep, in the water."

Rin underhand tossed the rock into the water. As the rock hit the surface the water splashed and rippled as the rock disappeared sinking to the bottom. Rin turned to Kim and saw she was holding an extremely satisfied look on her face.

"Now, what would you say if I asked you to go find that rock?" Kim asked her.

"I'd say no, that water's brown," Rin replied twisting her face.

"Exactly, no one would go in that water, especially not looking for a little silver rock right?"

"I-I guess not?"

"Then it'll stay there right?"

".... yeah?"

"Then that's how. No one's going in there to move that rock, no one but us even knows it's in there. That rock is gonna sit at the bottom of this swamp forever, and you, the last person to see or touch it, put it there. That's how easy one action can make a change that lasts forever."

Rin looked over to the water as she gathered words to speak.

"I mean…. OK, but that's just a rock in some water though," Rin claimed.

"Yeah, so? You still changed something. Next time go bigger. Toss a larger rock, or a tree branch. I'm not tryin to convince you that anyone will care or that you should even care about a rock at the bottom of a swamp. I'm just trying to show you that you have the ability to make changes in this world, both big and small, but you gotta do something first."

Rin looked back over at the water and a slight smile eventually came upon her face.

"Got it?" Kim asked.

"Yeah, got it," Rin nodded.

Kim stared at her curiously for a moment. Rin eventually noticed and raised an eyebrow.

"What's up?" she asked.

"Do you like it here?" Kim asked.

"Here? In this swamp?" Rin asked surprised by her question.

"No," Kim sucked her teeth at her, "I mean here in Joy City?"

"Oh, I mean, it's not the greatest place on earth I guess but my family's here so…"

"Yeah," Kim breathed looking back towards the water.

"Why, what's up?"

"Nothin, just curious. C'mon, let's get back inside." Kim shook her bandaged arm, "Need your help cleanin this."

Chapter 4

Relapse II

As Kim awoke out of her sleep, her heart rate skyrocketed. She hadn't yet gotten used to waking up staring at the pool hall's old wooden baseboards. As she pressed herself up onto her elbow, she groaned over a sharp pain emanating from her hip. Even with the extra cushion her sleeping bag provided, the wooden floors were still far from a mattress.

She scanned the pool hall and noticed she was alone inside. During the night the four of them rotated shifts where three would sleep as one stayed awake ensuring no one walked in on them while they were resting. Kim took the final shift after she and Rin came back inside and didn't end up going to sleep until nearly five in the morning. She had a splitting headache she assumed was due to a lack of rest. She reached for her cell phone laying on the floor next to her and unlocked it.

"8:42," the time on it read.

Still a bit groggy she contemplated lying back down to get another hour or two of rest. Her eyes shut as she yawned hard, and upon reopening them she was greeted by a huge smile.

"Morning sleepy head," Helena cheesed.

She was sitting with her legs crossed just mere inches from Kim.

"What is your obsession with invading my personal space?" Kim moaned.

"We're basically the same person, your space *is* my space," she grinned back.

Kim shot her an annoyed glare before standing to her feet. She braced herself up against the wall and began a full body stretch. She felt incredibly sore.

"Rin?!" she called out.

"They're all outside, they got up this morning with the sun while you laid there like a rock."

"I didn't get to sleep until like five," Kim sucked her teeth.

"Yeah yeah, excuses excuses." Helena said standing, "So, what's on today's agenda?"

"Survive. Yesterday was too quiet," Kim said.

"It was, good thing you think?"

"Knowing my life, no chance." she pushed herself off from the wall and headed outside.

"That's the spirit K!" Helena teased.

Kim rolled her eyes as she brushed aside the blue tarp hanging in front of the main entrance. She stepped outside and looked to her right where Rin, Aaliyah, and Charlotte all stood on the pool hall's porch.

"Oh look y'all, she's alive," Aaliyah said.

"Not for long, I'm on like three hours of sleep," Kim yawned.

"I'll take the night shift tonight," Aaliyah said.

"Well, what's the plan for today?" Kim asked stretching her spine.

"The plan for *right now* is get some food, we're all starving. We were waitin for you to wake up," Aaliyah said.

Kim hadn't eaten since yesterday afternoon when she was with Cindy. She was so tired her brain hadn't yet realized how hungry she was.

"And if we're gonna be stayin here, we might as well try to make it a bit more comfortable, pillows, extra blankets, a fan so we don't burn up in there at night," Charlotte added.

It suddenly hit Kim that they were living like fugitives, she couldn't believe it.

"We can get all that from the dollar store down the street," Aaliyah said.

"We all goin together or we splittin up or what?" Kim asked.

"Well, we got your car and Aaliyah's here, we could just all hop in one but if you're too tired you can stay here," Charlotte said.

Truthfully, she was too tired, but between hunger and the anxiety she had over their current situation, even if she did lay back down she knew she wouldn't be able to fall back asleep.

"No no. I'm fine, I'll go," she said rubbing her eyes.

Rin stepped forward. "If we got two cars here we might as well use them and make the trips easier and quicker for ourselves. We'll go to the store," she said nodding towards Kim, "and grab some stuff we can stock up on. Y'all go pickup whatever else we could use and get yourselves somethin to eat while you're out."

"Sounds like a plan," Aaliyah said, "grab some vegan-friendly stuff for me?"

"We gotchu," Rin assured her.

"Hey," Charlotte looked to Kim curiously, "you're not like wanted from that parking lot video last week are you?"

"Technically, probably, but the JCPD doesn't know who they're looking for. That video was so blurry it could've been anyone."

"Alright," Charlotte shrugged, "let's get movin then, my stomach's about to start eating itself. Stay alert, keep your eyes peeled, and watch each other's backs. Be safe."

"Always," Kim and Aaliyah responded in unison.

They both froze and stared at each other. Charlotte paused as well looking back and forth between them both. Their retired benediction, a long-forgotten force of habit, had left them all unsettled.

Rin looked at them puzzled by their shared spooked expressions. "Uhhh.... hey? Y'all good," she asked waving her hand, "what's wrong?"

Her voice snapped them all out of their trance.

"Yeah," Kim said shaking her head nervously, "let me grab my keys."

~

Kim pulled into the grocery store's parking lot and parked her car. She pulled the key out the ignition and fell back into her seat. She was exhausted. Mentally her mind was in disarray, physically she could barely keep her eyes open, her entire body was in pain from sleeping on the floor, and emotionally she felt like a caged animal.

"What's up?" Rin asked.

Kim looked over at her helplessly. "Is this real? Is this really our life right now? Gathering food to store in an abandoned pool hall where we crash on the floor? So paranoid one of us has to be awake at all times just to keep watch?"

"Right now, yes, what other options do we have?"

Kim exhaled in frustration.

"Hey," Rin nudged her, "it's alright, we're gonna figure this out. The good thing is no one's alone here."

With her mind in such a lock she wasn't able to voice it but she was truly grateful Rin was there. She wasn't sure if facing their current situation alone if she would still have hold of her sanity.

Rin's cell phone began buzzing in her pocket. She pulled it out and sucked her teeth as she read the caller ID.

"It's Hannah. If I don't answer she'll be on the way to my house in a minute."

"For what?"

"Nothin, she just likes to talk people's ear off. Now that she's jobless she's got twice as much time to. Go on in. I'll be in in a minute, my phone can never hold a signal inside that building."

"Alright," she handed Rin the keys, "lock it when you head in."

Rin nodded.

"Hey Hannah…." Rin answered her phone, "no no, I'm actually out with my sister. We're goin to visit some family."

Kim raised an eyebrow at her. She spit lies out just as quickly as she did herself, or used to rather. Kim stepped out the car and began making her way across the parking lot. As she walked she kept her eyes moving back and forth across the lot. Suddenly she felt an arm sling across the back of her neck and a body draw close to her. She gasped, looked to her side, and released a sigh of relief seeing Helena.

"You hear her?" Helena laughed, "Goin to visit family? I don't know if she lies as much as you but she's nowhere near as good at it as you are, or as you use to be at it anyway. One thing's for sure, you're definitely twins."

Kim lightly growled at her and the headache she was causing before shoving her away. She entered the store and claimed one of the empty carts. As she pushed it along, Helena stepped up onto the bottom rack of the cart.

"Awww man, this takes me back. Me and you, the grocery store, you shootin me that same nasty look, remember that night? Good times, good times," Helena smiled.

"Yeah, the day I began suffering from chronic migraines," Kim grumbled.

"Hey, you did it to yourself babe," she shrugged.

Kim made her way over to the produce area and opened a bag of grapes. She plucked a few from the cluster and popped them into her mouth.

"So, still no plan regarding the creepy snake-voiced guy hunting y'all down huh?" Helena asked.

"We can't do anything right now but lay low right? That's what you said."

"Yeah, but I didn't think you'd actually listen to me to be honest. I mean y'all can't just sit up in that pool hall forever."

Kim placed the bag of grapes into her cart.

"At the moment we don't have a choice," she said.

She continued walking about placing several bunches of fruit into her cart.

"OK, but at the same time what if whoever's hunting y'all snuffs out the pool hall? I mean eventually they gotta realize y'all aren't goin back to your houses, assuming they haven't already."

"Then we'll be ready," Kim replied harshly.

Kim cringed hearing herself utter the same answer she had judged Terrance for just days prior. Helena rolled her eyes.

"K, I love the confidence but..."

"Look," Kim stopped the cart, "we'll be fine. We've been in worse spots and made it out before."

"Alright alright," Helena breathed shaking her head.

"Get off so I can put some water under here," Kim said shaking the cart.

112

Helena stepped down from the cart's rack. Kim knelt down and placed four cases of bottled water on the rack. Her body ached and cracked each time she bent down. She slowly stood and tried to remember the list she and Rin had composed during the drive to the store.

"Hey, how bout a little of this?"

Kim turned around and saw Helena holding a bottle of wine.

"You might be able to fool everyone else but you know you can't lie to me. You're stressed out, a drink or two might do you some good?"

"I don't drink, put that down," Kim whispered to her.

"Ugh…. it's just wine Kim. You're no fun," Helena scoffed.

She placed the bottle back onto the shelf but only halfway. As she began to walk away the bottle tipped over, fell, and smashed into pieces as it hit the floor.

"Whoops," Helena whispered.

A few shoppers peeked their heads around the aisle to see the mess of wine and broken glass on the floor. Kim's face turned red with embarrassment.

"Really?" she grumbled at Helena through her teeth, "I told you to put it down."

"I did?" Helena cried.

Kim sucked her teeth at her and walked away searching for a store employee. She walked to the end of the aisle and looked both left and right but didn't see one. Though straight ahead of her she saw a door with a yellow sign on it that read,

"EMPLOYEES ONLY." She looked back down the aisle and eyed Helena furiously.

"Don't touch anything else," she mouthed to her.

Kim walked over to the door and peeked through the window but saw no one. She slowly pushed the door open and poked her head inside. It looked like a storage room for mostly canned goods and other items.

"Hello?" she called.

There was no answer. She pushed the door all the way open and pulled the stopper down with her foot. She took a few steps inside.

"Anyone who works here, there's some broken glass on aisle..."

The sound of a click immediately silenced her. She then felt something hard press up against the back of her head. The barrel of a gun. Kim slowly raised her hands.

"Where are the rest of you?" a feminine voice with a strong Polish accent asked.

She pressed the gun she was holding harder into the back of Kim's head.

"The rest of me?" Kim asked, "I think you have me confused with someone else..."

"The others, the ones in The Pool with you, where are they?"

Kim released a deeply distressed sigh. Just the mention of it stung. She couldn't deny it any longer.

"I don't know what you're talkin about..."

The woman pressed the gun even harder up against Kim's head. "Lies! You will tell me where they are!" the woman demanded.

Kim twisted her lips at her threat, "Or else what?" Kim asked.

She taunted the woman with her uninterested tone. She heard the woman snarl as she again rammed the gun into the back of her head.

"I'm going to count to three and…"

Another clicking sound immediately silenced the woman.

"That's cute, I'm gonna count to two," Rin said as she pressed a gun up to the back of the woman's head.

She pushed the door stopper back up with her foot allowing it to close behind her. Rin grabbed the woman's arm and pulled it to the side taking the gun from her. Kim dropped her hands and turned around to face them. Rin tossed the gun to her which she caught and pressed into the woman's stomach. She looked at her and saw the cold scowl on her face. She had full pink lips and large blue eyes which held hatred in them.

"Hands up," Kim told her.

The woman flared her nostrils at Kim.

"I'd do what she says, she's not in the best of moods right now," Rin said over the woman's shoulder.

She slowly raised her hands in submission. Kim raised the gun tucking the barrel right under the woman's chin.

"Who sent you?" Kim asked.

"I do not answer to you, he will have his revenge whether you kill me or not," the woman responded.

"It's just us sweetheart, you can drop the dramatic act," Rin teased.

"Wait, *he*? Who is *he*? And what revenge?" Kim asked.

The woman refused to answer. Rin looked down and her eyes lit up. She reached down at the woman's waist.

"Kim," Rin said as she held up another voice recorder identical to the others.

"Play it," Kim said.

Rin pressed the circular button and it begin playing.

"I'm enjoyin hearin about you girls squirmin. And what luck, Kim's twin sister, who must obviously have a death wish, has decided to join in on the fun as well. I don't mind killin one more of you, the sweeter the retribution. And the best part, you're all gonna walk yourselves right into your own demise searching for answers. You can start at Joy City's highest point, abstain from it, and more'll just keep comin."

Kim and Rin made brief eye contact as the recording ended. Kim pressed the gun harder into the woman's chin.

"Who's the voice on the tape, what is he talkin about?" Kim demanded.

"I do not answer to you, he will have his revenge, you will suffer," the woman repeated.

"With all due respect, that's not in the cards," Rin said.

Kim thought for a moment, attempting to connect the dots but still couldn't. She looked back at Rin and nodded. Kim tucked the gun into the back of her pants and stepped from in front of the woman. Rin pushed her forward a bit keeping the gun pointed at the back of her head.

"Move it princess." Rin said, "Grab enough of whatever to last us a few days, we need to meet back up with Aaliyah and Charlotte. I'll deal with her and meet you back at the car."

Kim nodded as Rin handed her her keys. Rin walked the woman to the back of the storage room and out the back door. Kim exited back out the door she entered and walked over to her cart. Stepping over the wine spill, she headed straight for the register to check out.

After she finished inside the store she walked outside and crossed the parking lot with bags in each of her hands. As she got closer to her car she noticed a boy who looked to be in his late teens down on his knees buffing her car door with an old rag. She walked up and stood behind him.

"Ummm…. excuse me?"

The boy looked up and immediately stood upon seeing Kim.

"Oh, hello. I-I'm sorry, is this…"

"Yeah, my car, what are you doing?" she asked.

"Just givin it a quick shine," the boy smiled.

Something about him made her skin crawl. Whether it was his crooked smile, his pale freckled face, or his shaky voice, she couldn't tell what but something about him just didn't sit right with her.

"If-if you want, I could do the windows too I..."

Kim reached into her back pocket and pulled out a twenty-dollar bill.

"Here kid," she said holding the bill out to him, "just go."

The boy's eyes lit up as he took the money, thanked her, and walked away. Kim rested the grocery bags and the gun she had tucked into her pants in the backseat. She then slumped down behind the steering wheel. Taking several slow deep breaths, she attempted to calm herself down. Suddenly a loud bang caused her to jump in her seat. She looked back towards the store and sighed. The sound of someone whistling came from her backseat. She looked up at the rearview mirror and saw Helena grinning at her.

"Yeah, Charlotte definitely taught her a thing or two, she's not who she was four years ago," she laughed.

Kim sunk deeper into her seat. Helena leaned forward over the center console and looked at Kim. She held a hopeless look on her face. She looked absolutely defeated. Helena lightly nudged her shoulder.

"Hey, c'mon, don't do that. It's gonna be OK," she assured her.

Kim didn't speak nor move. Helena sighed and quietly sat back without another word. About a minute later Rin came walking out from the store's main entrance. She walked around to the passenger door, opened it, and nonchalantly sat inside. She reached behind her back and pulled the gun she had and held it out for Kim to take. Kim looked at her confused for a moment.

"It's yours," she said, "found it under the seat."

Kim took the gun from her and rested it in her lap.

"Keep that on you, at this point we can't tell where or when these people are comin," Rin said.

"This isn't enough though," Kim said looking down at the gun.

"No, it's not…. so?"

Kim looked up at her.

"Call one of them. Tell them to watch themselves and get back to the pool hall as soon as possible."

~

Kim pulled into the driveway of her house. She tucked her chain, reached into the backseat, grabbed the gun she had taken from the woman at the store, and handed it to Rin. They both exited the car and slowly walked up to her front door, frantically looking in every direction as they approached the house.

Once at the front door Kim placed her hand on the knob and gently tried to turn it. The door was locked. She was relieved. She put her key into the door and slowly turned it until it unlocked. Rin stepped up next to her and gently nodded. Kim gave a slight nod back and then quickly turned the knob shouldering through the door. She took a single step into the house holding the gun out in front of her. She quickly scanned over everything in her sight. The house was quiet and appeared to be empty, just as she had left it.

"Stay in the doorway, I'mma sweep the place," Kim whispered to Rin.

Rin nodded. Kim began to carefully tip toe through the house. She crept into the kitchen making note of the mountain of unwashed dishes she had left in the sink. She passed through the kitchen and peeked around the corner into the living room. She saw her four throw pillows and blanket spread out about the couch as she remembered leaving them.

She backed out the living room, passed back through the kitchen, and headed upstairs. Taking slow soft steps up the incline, she was careful not to make too much noise. When she reached the top, she inched over to her guest room and pushed the door open to take a quick glance inside; it was clear. She made her way over to Cindy's room, opened the door and saw it also looked fine. Lastly, she peeked into her own room, and saw everything in its place as well. She let out a sigh of relief. It felt like her first lucky break in days. She walked back over to the top of the staircase and looked down at Rin standing in the doorway.

"Looks clear. Keep an eye out. I'll be down in a minute," Kim told her.

Rin again nodded. Kim backed into her room and walked into her closet. She pulled out two duffle bags, one open and empty and one zipped up bulging at the sides from whatever was in it. She placed both of them on her bed and knelt down by her nightstand. She pulled out the bottom two drawers, dumped their contents onto the bed, and flipped the drawers completely over. Taped to the bottom of the drawers were three handguns, several cases of ammunition, and a few knives and daggers. She ripped through the tape that bound them to the drawers and placed them into the empty duffle bag and then unzipped the other bag and looked inside. It was stuffed full of several stacks of hundred-dollar bills bound by rubber bands. The money had been sitting in the bag for years; it was her rainy-day stash. She didn't actually know how much was inside the bag, though she remembered she had stopped counting after about three hundred thousand, and the bag was only half full then. *Just in case,* she thought to herself.

She zipped both bags up and tossed the one holding the weapons over her shoulder. She lifted the other up from the bed and heard something hit the floor. She dropped the bag back onto the bed, looked down, and saw her purple hair pick lying at her feet.

Something about seeing it made her body go numb. She dropped the other bag from her shoulder onto the floor and slowly bent over. She took the pick up from the floor and held it in front of her face. She examined it closely. It had been so long since she had held it in her hand for more than just a second, years since she had walked out the house with it on her.

She ran her thumb over the slightly embossed flower design as gruesome visions of her past suddenly rushed through her mind. The places she had been with it tucked at her waist; the things she had done with it gripped tightly in her hand.

"Welp, it's official…"

Kim looked over and saw Helena standing in the doorway. Her smile arrogant and condemning as ever.

"…. you're back," she smiled.

Kim eyed over to the tall pillar that rose over the mirror of her dresser and noticed Helena's beanie wasn't hanging where she had left it four years ago. She had paid so little mind to it over the years she wasn't able to remember if she had taken it down herself at one point or if it had still been there four days ago when she was last home. She let the thought pass and then looked back at the pick. She felt a lump form in her throat. Helena's words felt like the truth she wasn't ready to accept. Helena walked forward stopping just inches from where she stood.

"You still remember how to use that thing?" she asked, "I'm thinkin you might need to pretty soon."

Kim quickly flipped the pick around in her hand and released its blade in between her fingers. Helena smiled deviously at the sight.

"Like the last four years never even happened," she giggled.

Kim retracted the blade and tucked the pick at her waist. It felt cold and unfamiliar pressed up against her skin sending shivers down her spine. She grabbed the bag up from the floor and threw it back over her shoulder and picked the other up from the bed carrying it at her side. Without so much as a word or even a quick glance she walked past Helena and headed out the room.

"Kim," Helena called to her.

She stopped but didn't turn around to face her.

"It's gonna be OK," Helena said softly.

Kim sighed, dropped her head, and walked out the room, down the stairs. She poked her head out the door and motioned for Rin to step inside. Kim opened the bag holding the weapons and Rin dropped the gun she was holding inside.

"Both of these full of weapons?" Rin asked.

"No, just one. The other is some cash to last us a while in case we need it."

She threw the bag back over her shoulder and ushered Rin back outside. They walked back to the car carefully surveying every direction around them. Kim pulled the car door open and placed both bags in the backseat with the groceries. She then slid back behind the driver seat.

"So, what now?" Rin asked.

"What'd that recording say, the city's highest point or something?" Kim asked.

"Yeah, something like that," Rin reached into her pocket, "I got it right here."

"I don't think we should follow it. We should probably just try to lay low like Terrance said, but still it'll be good if we can..."

Kim paused mid-sentence as a small steady beeping sound caught her ear. Rin froze as well.

"Is that the car?" Rin asked.

"I don't think so, it's not even on," Kim said holding up the keys.

They both began looking carefully over the dashboard yet couldn't find the source. Suddenly the beeping began to ramp up. Both Kim and Rin's eyebrows raised as they began looking all around the car for where the noise was coming from. Kim turned around and looked into the backseat but couldn't figure out what it was.

"Is it something in the bag?" Rin asked.

"No, I just put a few handguns and blades in there."

The beeping began to speed up even more. Sounding with hardly any pause in between its chirps. It had turned from a single beep to what sounded like an alert or alarm that had been triggered. Worried looks struck Kim and Rin's faces as they both had the same horrifying thought.

"Get out of the car!" Kim demanded.

Rin immediately opened her door and jumped out of the car. Kim reached behind her seat and grabbed the strap of one of the duffle bags. She yanked it into her lap.

"Get back! Get away from it!" she yelled over her shoulder to Rin.

Kim rolled out of the car but the strap of the bag got caught on the corner of the door and pulled her back. She pulled hard at the strap and it broke sending her stumbling backwards. She landed hard on her side in the grass. Suddenly a loud boom shook the ground beneath her and a pillar of smoke and flames shot up through the roof of her car. All four of the car's doors blew off in separate directions as well as the trunk and hood. The windows shattered and blasted shards of glass all over the lawn and into the street. Other pieces of debris shot up into the sky before crashing back down.

Kim waved her arm out in front of her trying to clear the smoke impairing her vision. Once the smoke cleared she saw only the flaming charred frame of the car still intact. She was dumbstruck.

She rolled over and grabbed the bag she had snatched out the car and unzipped it. She looked inside and saw it was the one stuffed with cash. She sucked her teeth.

"Kim?! Kim?!" Rin called in a panic as she ran up and dropped down to a knee next to her, "You alright?"

"Yeah," Kim grunted pushing herself up.

They both stood for a second looking at the car's remains scattered about in a muddled awe.

"What just happened?!" Rin cried.

Kim's look of confusion then transformed into one full of rage.

"That kid at the store!" she hissed through clenched teeth and fiery eyes.

"What?" Rin asked, "what kid?"

Kim didn't answer, she was fuming as she stared at the mess on her lawn.

"Kim?"

"Forget what Terrance said. We're done hiding. We're done laying low. If this guy wants to see us, he's gonna see us."

Chapter 5

Desire

Kim dropped a water hose to the ground and stomped over to the side of her house. She twisted the valve on the spigot until the water ceased flowing.

"Cabs are pullin up!" Rin called to her from the street.

Kim dried her hands off on her pants as she walked towards her.

"Did you get one of them on the phone?" Kim asked her.

"Yeah, talked to Charlotte. Told her we had a…. happening, and that they need to get back to the pool hall ASAP. Told them to ditch Aaliyah's car, call a cab, and trash their cell phones. I'mma head to the nearest place I can find some burner phones and grab a few."

"I'll grab one for myself before I head back. When you get yours, text my cell and I'll hit you back on the burner."

Two yellow taxi cabs pulled up near the sidewalk leading to Kim's driveway.

"Where are you goin?" Rin asked.

"To get a car. We can't afford to be waiting on cabs, we're gonna need somethin we can jump in at a moment's notice if we need to, and right now I don't trust that Aaliyah's car isn't being tracked."

"From where, that old junkyard?" Rin asked.

"No, that junkyard was sold about a year ago and the new owner gated it off. I'm gonna have to go buy one."

"That's gonna take forever."

"No, I know a guy. I'll be in and out in thirty minutes."

One of the cab drivers laid on his horn.

"Alright alright, comin!" Rin waved towards the car, "Anything else?"

Kim looked off to the side thinking for a moment.

"Call Charlotte back before they get rid of their phones and tell them to swing by their houses and grab anything they have we could use to protect ourselves cause we just lost everything we had."

"Everything?" Rin huffed with wide eyes.

Kim bent over and unzipped the bag of money resting at her feet. Rin looked inside and sighed despairingly at the sight. They would've both liked for her to have grabbed the one full of weapons rather than cash.

"Yeah," Kim frowned up at her, "my luck..."

Kim zipped the bag up and stuffed it under her arm. "Text me as soon as you can," she said.

"Wait, you just gonna leave your car and its parts all spread out over your lawn like this?" Rin asked looking at the scattered wreckage.

"The fire's out," she shrugged, "it's hardly the worst-looking lawn on the block, even now. It'll blend right in."

~

"C'mon Rin, hurry up," Kim mumbled to herself.

She was holding her cell phone and a burner phone she had just bought waiting for a text to come through from Rin. She was sitting inside of a car dealership, one she knew well, waiting to be helped.

She looked around anxiously, tapping her foot, unsure of what she was even keeping an eye out for.

"Fitting I pop back into existence and almost immediately stuff starts blowing up."

Kim rolled her eyes at the comment. Helena jumped down from the large counter she was sitting on and sat in the chair next to Kim.

"You and trouble just can't seem to stay out of each other's way huh?" Helena shrugged.

"Had a good run for about four years but…. you know…" Kim mumbled, staring at the phones.

"Yeah, but four years is just four years K. We can do better, we should want better."

Kim found her statement almost insulting, as if Helena were implying she didn't want better.

"Little Kim!" a tall Hispanic man in a white dress shirt, black slacks, and a tie greeted her as he approached.

He had bronzed skin and black slicked back

hair. Kim slid both phones into her pocket and pushed herself up to greet the man with an embrace.

"Haven't been little in a while but still Kim. How you been Tony?" Kim smiled.

Tony was the owner of a small, privately owned car dealership in Joy City. His father founded it but after his passing it fell into Tony's hands. His father and Kim's foster father were great friends, and while growing up Kim and him never spent much time around each other they were still well acquainted. Tony was nearly ten years older than Kim and never grew out of calling her "Little Kim," the name she was first introduced to him as when she was only seven years old.

"Good, just tryin to make a livin out here," he shrugged smiling back.

"Aren't we all?" Kim said.

"So, what's up? Haven't seen you since…"

"Since I bought Cindy that car a few years back."

"That's right, how's she doin?"

"Good, she's in college now, makin it."

"Good, good, so how bout you? It's been so long…. well, maybe that's a good thing," he laughed.

Tony and his father played a vital role in The Pool without really knowing it themselves. Kim wasn't entirely sure how much they knew but she knew they didn't know the specifics of what The Pool was or what those inside it did. What they did do was provide unregistered vehicles to the members of The Pool when they needed them.

Joy City's three unspoken rules; live with

129

somebody worth dying for, get some money, and stay out the way. Tony and his father were prime examples of those who lived by these rules. So long as The Pool members paid a little extra on top, they never asked any questions. The dirt they were doing was none of their business, they chose to stay out of the way and just take the money.

"Well, actually, I'm here for exactly what you think," Kim said.

She gently kicked the duffle bag full of money resting on the floor. Tony smiled and shook his head.

"Wrecked another one?" he laughed.

It had become a running gag between them how many cars Kim had bought off the lot over the years.

"Somethin like that," Kim shrugged.

"Well, I got some bad news kid, we're packing up today. Shipping our whole inventory out of JC tomorrow and we can't have so much as a hubcap missing when it all touches down."

"What? Shipping where? Y'all goin out of business?"

"Nope, merging with another lot." he leaned up against the counter and grinned, "Expanding. It was Pop's dream to grow this place into something bigger one day and we finally found the right opportunity to do it. Took all these years but I'd like to think he'd be proud of me, proud I haven't run the place into the ground."

"He would be proud..." Kim nodded, ".... he *is* proud."

"Thanks. It'll also be good just to get out of

this city, you know? Hard to believe this place has been as bad as it's been for so long. It's stressful runnin a brick and mortar here. You never know, you wake up one morning and everything you worked for could go up in flames, like that gym the other day."

"Yeah…. you know Charlotte owned that place?"

"What? Really?" Tony's eyes lit up.

Kim nodded.

"Is she OK?" he asked.

"She's fine. I mean, she's a little emotionally scarred at the moment but she's OK."

Tony heaved a deep sigh. The toll the city took on those who lived inside it was truly awful. It had become too normal seeing people look down at their feet and just shake their heads in disappointment.

"Well, anyway kid, I'm sorry I can't get you in a car today. Had you showed up about twenty-four hours earlier we might've been able to work something out but we're loading cars in like two hours."

"You don't have anything? I'll take a beater, I just need four wheels, brakes, and an engine right now."

"Everything's gotta go sweetheart. If one bolt is missin they can dead the whole merge and we'll be screwed."

Kim sighed and bit her lip.

"The new lot's only two cities over, we'll be up and running by next week if you can wait. But I gotta be honest with you, I can't guarantee you a sale without registration over there, at least not yet. Let me get my foot in the door and feel things out first, and I'll let you know."

"No…. no, don't risk a good business opportunity on me. You won't be in Joy City anymore, don't take any of this place's bad habits with you. Plus, I need something today anyway, so…"

Kim bent over, picked up the duffle bag of money and slung it over her shoulder. She looked into Tony's eyes and smiled. She was happy to see someone make it out, see someone start in Joy City and find an honest path that led away from it. She thought about Cindy's request the day before, hoping she would soon be so lucky to find a path out as well.

"Good luck, thanks for everything," she said hugging him tight.

"How much are you willing to spend?" he asked before letting her go.

Kim drew back a bit, "What do you mean?"

He looked around cautiously and lowered his tone to a whisper.

"If you're willing and able to spend a little more than usual I can get you in something today."

"Ummm…. you sure? I don't wanna ruin anything for you," Kim whispered.

"All the money you spent here over the years, consider it one last favor for helping me feed my family all this time."

"I need four doors," Kim said.

"Four doors or four seats?" he asked with a smug look.

Kim cut her eyes and cocked her head at him;

132

he had her attention. He motioned for her to follow him. They exited out the back of the dealership and walked over to the service garage. Tony unlocked the door, peeked inside, and ushered Kim in after him. He quickly locked the door back behind her. Kim took a quick glance around and noticed the garage was completely empty except for a single car covered by a white tarp. Tony began a slow stroll towards it. Kim followed behind him.

"I went through hell trying to get this thing here. No dealer wants to send anything to Joy City because, well…. they know it's Joy City. They don't believe anyone here can afford anything over thirty grand but I begged and pleaded for just one and eventually they caved. They agreed to send it last Friday, they dropped it off yesterday, Monday, but I sent off our inventory paperwork two days before they shipped it."

"OK, so…" Kim began.

"So *this* wasn't on there, the car's a ghost. No tags, it's not registered to an operating lot, and there are no records of it getting ready to be transferred to one."

Kim looked at the tarp and saw curves and sharp edges poking out. There was something exotic underneath.

"How much?" Kim asked.

With a devilish grin Tony grabbed the tarp and tore it away. Kim cut her eyes and cursed under her breath as she looked over the vehicle. She had never seen anything like it before, not in Joy City.

"She a beauty or what?" Tony smirked.

Helena suddenly appeared on Kim's right gazing starry eyed at the vehicle.

She cheesed in approval, "K, give the man the money before he changes his mind."

~

Helena whistled aloud as she fiddled with the dash instruments.

"I'm proud of you K, you're finally startin to listen to me. You can't take all your money with you when you're gone, you might as well splurge a little bit while you still got the chance."

Kim batted her hands away from the buttons and nobs she was messing with. She was already kicking herself for caving in to something so material, and Helena fawning over the car only made her feel worse about the decision. She charged it to the last four years of her life rather than a complete lack of mental fortitude. Living in peace for so long had softened her up a bit, and she hated it.

"Can you not!" she scoffed as she drove, "I'm already regretting it. As soon as things calm down I'm getting rid of it, so stop messin with stuff."

"What?! Why?!" Helena cried.

"Because I don't need it."

Kim hushed as she felt a vibration in her pocket. She pulled out her cell phone and saw a text from an unsaved number. The text was a phone number.

"Rin," she whispered to herself.

She pulled out the burner phone she had

bought and began copying over the number.

"You're gonna text and drive uninsured behind the wheel of this?" Helena asked. "K, if you get in a wreck…"

"Shut up," Kim hushed her.

She placed the burner phone in between her shoulder and cheek. It rang twice before Rin answered.

"Hello?"

"Hey."

"Hey, you get a car?"

Helena snatched the phone and shouted into it with a huge smile on her face, "Oh she got more than a car sis!"

Kim violently snatched the phone back and mean mugged her. She put the phone on speaker and dropped it into her lap.

"Yeah, I got one. Did Aaliyah and Charlotte get any weapons?"

"Not really. Aaliyah had a knife she kept from years ago but that's about it."

Kim cursed under her breath. Even after the fall of The Pool she kept all the weapons she had in her home to protect herself if need be. She couldn't imagine why they wouldn't have done the same.

"Sheesh, y'all really can't catch a break," Helena said kicking her feet up on the dashboard.

"Maybe we ask Terrance, I'm sure he…"

"No," Kim said, cutting Rin off, "we need to stay as far away from him as possible. There's a good chance someone's gonna be sent his way too, but if not, we don't wanna put anyone else in danger, bad enough we stopped there when we did."

"Yeah, right…. well, hey I told Aaliyah and Charlotte about the recording and we were tryin to figure out what he was talkin about, you know the whole highest point thing or whatever?"

"Yeah?"

"What about that hill you use to go up to all the time? It was pretty high, right?"

With so many things happening so fast Kim hadn't yet taken a moment to really think about the last recording's cryptic clue.

"The city's highest point?" she whispered to herself, "Yeah…. yeah I guess. Could be."

"Should we check it out?" Rin asked.

Kim discreetly eyed over towards Helena. She held an orgulous grin on her face as she side-eyed Kim back; the answer she was looking for.

"The three of you be on the corner of Comet, I'll be there in ten minutes."

"Wait, you wanna go now? Like with no weapons?"

"It's better than just sitting around with no weapons, he said if we didn't come more people would just keep comin for us."

Kim heard Rin release a sigh of grief. She could sense she was unsure about the move.

"Just be on comet when I get there OK?"

"Alright," Rin said.

Kim hung up and tucked the burner phone into her pocket. She took her cell phone and quickly snapped it in half tossing the two pieces out the window. She put her focus back on the road in front of her and shook her head in disbelief.

"You know it's a trap right?" Helena said gazing out the window.

"Of course it is," Kim grumbled.

Helena leaned back in her seat and placed her hands behind her head.

"But you're still gonna march right up there into it aren't you?"

Kim's nostrils flared and she tightened her grip on the steering wheel.

"Of course you are," Helena giggled to herself.

~

Kim pulled up on the shoulder of Comet street where Rin, Aaliyah, and Charlotte were waiting and stopped the car. She stepped out and froze noticing them all staring at her in awe.

"What?" Kim asked shrugging.

"Uhhh…. Kim, when you said you got a car…" Rin began.

Kim rolled her eyes.

"It's a long story alright, it just kinda happened. C'mon, we need to go."

"Hold up," Aaliyah said admiring the car, "this is next year's model, this ain't even out yet. What was one of these even doin in Joy City?"

"I don't know, look can we…"

"Fresh from the factory too," Charlotte added, "they didn't let this off the lot for anything less than one-fifty."

Charlotte pushed the driver seat forward and

jumped in the back seat. Aaliyah followed in behind her.

"Sheesh Kim, you didn't have to one up us like this," Charlotte said.

"Right? She got fancy on us," Aaliyah grinned as she eyed around, "I might just have to cash out for one of these myself. This is nice."

Kim twisted her lips at them marveling over the car. Normally she would scold them for praising something so material but she was in fact the one who bought it.

"Hey, I know you got it but is there a reason? I mean we're tryin to lay low right?" Rin asked her.

Kim shook her head and silently cursed Helena and then herself for listening to her. She quickly shed the thoughts to regain her focus.

"It's…. complicated. Look, we need to go, get in."

"Wait, do we even have a plan?"

"No Rin!" Kim snapped at her, "We don't! Someone just threatened to send more people to kill us the longer we try to hide, so time's really not on our side right now. If we can't figure a plan out by the time we get there we're just gonna have to wing it."

The bass in Kim's voice coupled with a harsh glare caused Rin to cower back a bit. While it was a rare happening during their short time of knowing each other, Kim made it clear she was not afraid to assert her dominance as the older sister when she felt she needed to.

"OK OK." Rin whispered, as she walked

around to the passenger side of the car.

As she walked Kim noticed her feet dragging, her shoulders slumped down, her head hanging low, and her bottom lip tucked. She hated feeling like she was barking at her but she also felt it necessary in the moment. In her mind she was just trying to keep them all alive; Rin could get over being yelled at, she had plenty of times before. Kim quickly shook the thought, got in the car, and headed for The Hill.

~

Kim stepped over a small shrub and froze. She carefully scanned left and right looking out for anything abnormal. She listened as the wind whipped the leaves of the large oak tree resting on the hilltop. The site appeared just as calm and peaceful as it always had for years.

"Looks clear," Kim whispered over her shoulder, "keep your eyes and ears peeled."

Rin, Aaliyah, and Charlotte were close behind, clinging to the steep incline they were climbing. Kim slowly continued to step until she stood on almost flat land. Her eyes continued to drift all around.

"I think we're alone," Charlotte said.

"Maybe," Kim said.

"You use to climb this daily? This is a whole workout," Aaliyah gasped.

"Not daily, but enough," Kim replied.

The four of them walked forward until they stood at the edge of the cliff overlooking the city.

"I see why though," Aaliyah said as her eyes

grew wide, "some view. Never seen JC from this high up. From here it almost looks like a place worth living."

Kim hadn't been to the top of The Hill in a while. In fact, she couldn't remember having walked up it at all in the past two years. It was her place to think, unwind, and escape her life's woes when she needed to. However, the last few years of her life had been relatively stress-free. There was nothing to escape from. What surprised her was that The Hill seemed exactly as it had the last time she remembered standing atop it. Everything from the sights to the sounds felt familiar. She wondered how many people other than Rin and herself had ever actually climbed it?

"Yeah yeah, the view's nice and all but why are we here?" Charlotte asked.

"The recording said to come to the highest point, this would be it wouldn't it?" Rin shrugged.

"Come for what though?" Charlotte asked.

Kim tuned them both out as they continued talking amongst each other. She looked out across the cityscape deeply analyzing everything in sight. She didn't know exactly what she was looking for but figured she would know it when she saw it.

"You know…"

A sharp pain suddenly struck Kim's head. She winced and discreetly looked back over her shoulder and saw Helena walking towards the cliff's edge with her hands behind her head.

"… I'm thinkin dude might be just runnin y'all on a wild goose chase K. He told you to come here, but didn't say why or for what, and then he's not even here when you show up?"

Kim turned her head back around as Helena continued to walk towards the edge. She bit the inside of her jaw and flared her nostrils as the same thought had already crossed her mind a few times.

"I'm just sayin, what if this little field trip was just a distraction?" Helena suggested, "What if he's just tryin to keep you guessin so while you're busy tryin to decipher his warnings and threats you fall blind to something right in front of..."

An ear-piercing screech suddenly filled the air, followed by the sound of rattling chains, and then a loud thud. Kim looked back over her shoulder and her eyes immediately locked on Helena who was looking down at her feet where a thin circular object attached to a steel chain with six karambit-curved blades protruding from its sides had struck the ground right in front of her. Rin, Aaliyah, and Charlotte all turned around and stared at the object. Kim looked up at Helena. Even she held a disoriented look on her face.

"Uhhh…. that's not mine," Helena shrugged.

The chain attached to the object began to rattle again. Kim noticed it was exceptionally long and led behind where Helena stood until it rose and disappeared up into the foliage of the large oak tree. Looking up, Kim squinted and noticed a patch of leaves suddenly begin shifting. A figure unfolded and dropped to the ground, landing in a crouched position near the tree's base. The figure stood and froze; it was obviously the build of a man. Everyone's eyes were glued on him. He wore a light green kimono with a leaf pattern printed all over it. His face was covered by a mask pulled up over his nose, and on his head he wore a large straw kasa.

"Look at this clown." Helena giggled, "Sorry dude, you missed feudal Japan by a few hundred years!"

The end of the chain attached to the object was wrapped several times around his right arm. In one lightning fast move he grabbed at the hanging part of the chain and snatched it across his body. The circular object quickly zipped from the ground towards him making the same horrible screeching noise it had before. The blades sticking out spun wildly as it cut through the air. Just as it came inches from him, he caught it barehanded, grasping a small indentation in its top.

"This our guy?" Charlotte asked.

"What is he holding?" Aaliyah asked.

"Looks like some kinda weapon.... some kinda spinning wheel with blades attached?" Rin suggested.

Kim looked at the man in wonder. His attire told her he couldn't have been from Joy City, not originally at least. Though if he was the one leaving the recordings he knew her foster parents, and so he at least had been in the city well over a decade ago. She turned her head to her left and saw Rin, Aaliyah, and Charlotte looking at her waiting for her word. She looked back at the man and took a small step forward.

"Are you the person who's been…"

Before she could get her question out he

charged forward, bee-lining for her.

"Move!" Kim gasped pushing Rin away from her.

She quickly tucked her chain into her shirt and stepped forward putting some space in between herself and the cliff's edge. She then braced herself in a fighting stance. With the circular object held in his left hand he spun the loose end of the chain in his other in a circle as he dashed towards her. When he was just inches from her, he swung the chain upwards at an angle which she evaded with a lean backwards. He then pulled the chain back down at an angle under which Kim ducked. She came up quickly and landed a left hook across his face. He responded swinging the bladed weapon at her but another backwards lean put her out of his reach. She attempted to counter with a right hook but her strike was blocked as he raised his arm back up. She ended up punching the weapon he was holding; it was cold and hard to the touch. He then swung a right hook that landed and caused Kim to stumble backwards. The chain wrapped around his arm made the blow heavier. Before she could regain her stance, the man shot the chain's end out and it connected with her shin. She winced and immediately collapsed to a knee.

He pulled the chain back but before he could make another move Aaliyah shouldered into his back knocking him away from Kim. With some distance between the two of them she pulled her knife and stared the man down waiting for him to make a move. He quickly shot the chain towards Aaliyah just as he had at Kim. Aaliyah put her forearm out to block the blow but was surprised when the end of the chain wrapped around the blade of her knife. With a single tug of the chain he ripped the knife from her grasp and whipped it away over the cliff's edge.

"OK.... checkmate," Aaliyah whispered to herself.

He began spinning the weapon at his side as he stared Aaliyah down. He took a single step forward and kicked it out of its spin straight towards her. Shrieking horribly, it spun, shredding over the grass with blistering speed. Aaliyah jumped to her left and out the way as it ripped past her. The man grabbed the chain, yanked it back, and then pulled it across his body redirecting it back towards her. She immediately dove to the ground and rolled as it passed just inches above her head. Tumbling along the grass, she crashed into the base of the oak tree. She looked over to Charlotte standing a few feet away who was equally awestricken.

Rin then charged the man, swinging a wild hook which he blocked with his forearm while catching the weapon in his other hand. He slashed it down but she evaded it and delivered a quick jab to his stomach. He responded throwing a left uppercut that missed, and then another swing of the weapon that zipped above Rin's head. They traded a series of jabs and crosses, neither landing much, until Rin threw one a little too high. He ducked under her left arm and threw a heavy elbow into her ribcage. Trying to correct herself she threw a wild right that missed by so much she stumbled forward a bit. He punished her with another hard elbow strike to her back. With Rin stunned, he crouched and swung his leg low sweeping her off her feet. She hit the ground hard. He stood looking down on her as she held her back.

"Hey!" Charlotte yelled as she rushed him.

Without looking he threw the weapon out and spun in place with it rotating about a yard's length around him. Charlotte had to collapse to her knees and slide to avoid the swing. As he caught the weapon again she immediately rose and threw a cross-body punch that missed. She immediately brought her fist back attempting to strike him backhanded but he leaned away evading it as well. She threw one more hook that he wiped away with his forearm and countered with an open palm strike to her gut. The impact knocked the breath out of her. She threw a weak slow jab that allowed him to grab her arm, yank her forward, and sweep her feet out from under her. He effortlessly tossed her backwards where she landed a few feet in front of Kim. Charlotte held her stomach as she groaned. He stood over her and raised the weapon up over his head.

"Charlotte move!" Kim yelled.

Charlotte immediately rolled backwards just as he slammed the weapon's blades into the ground.

Rin again charged at him, this time loudly snarling through clenched teeth. Before she could even get close to him he again spun in place swinging the weapon around himself at an even greater radius than before. Rin had to stop and immediately prone to avoid being hit.

"Hey!" Kim yelled over to her, "stay back!"

145

He caught the weapon and stared all three of them down. His demeanor was so placid it was daunting, as if downing them hadn't caused him to even break a sweat. They were all dumbfounded. None of them had ever seen such a weapon wielded in such a way.

"Hey!" Aaliyah called from behind him.

He turned his head around slightly acknowledging her. She picked up a medium-sized branch that had fallen from the oak tree.

"They're down, it's you and me again."

She heaved the branch hard towards him. Before it got halfway to him, he turned around and threw the weapon at the branch slicing it in half. He redirected it up and over his head and it landed sticking into the ground just inches from Charlotte's feet.

"Tsk.... showoff," Aaliyah quietly mumbled.

He began slowly walking Aaliyah down, dragging the chain behind himself. Kim scanned the hill looking for options. She suddenly remembered she had grabbed her pick before leaving her house. She rose and dashed at him. In one fluid motion she pulled the pick from her side, released the blade, and tried to stab him in the back. At the same time the chain suddenly detached near his hand and he quickly ducked under Kim's arm and spun around to her back. He pulled about a foot of the chain from around his arm and took the loose end in his other hand. He wrapped it tightly around Kim's neck, spun around, and pulled her up and over his back dumping her hard onto the ground. She landed awkwardly on her left shoulder and had to bite her lip to keep from screaming.

"What is this guy?" Aaliyah breathed as she watched in horror.

Rin could do nothing but hold her breath at the sight. The man stood over Kim looking down at her; his silence was menacing. He bent over and grabbed her pick up from the ground. He began twirling it in his hands in a taunting fashion. Kim slowly rolled over onto her back grabbing at her neck. The chain left a bright red imprint on her skin. She looked up imagining if she could see his face he would have had a hideously haughty smirk across it. She couldn't recall ever feeling so outmatched in a fight, especially one where she had a numbers advantage. She began to question ever calling herself an assassin, this man was a *real* assassin. Compared to him she felt like nothing more than a street brawler.

Standing over her, he continued twirling the pick in his hand, but he suddenly stopped, looked up, and froze. Kim heard the sound of a rattling chain behind her. She spun her head around and saw Charlotte up on one knee holding the man's weapon.

"OK pendejo, I've had just about enough of you," she huffed.

She crossed her body and hurled the weapon towards him. It passed directly over Kim's head as the man simply sidestepped to avoid the attack. The weapon's blades stuck high into the oak tree's trunk. Charlotte held tightly onto the end of the chain while still crouched on one knee. They were locked in an intense stare down. He slowly stepped around Kim, gripped the pick tightly in his hand, and fell into a sprint in Charlotte's direction. He took three steps before Charlotte snatched the chain back. The weapon screamed as it came flying out of the tree towards the man's back. He halted his dash, turned his head, and before he knew it, it was severed.

The Hill fell silent. Not so much as a light breath could be heard. Charlotte collapsed to her hands and knees right next to where the weapon's blades stuck into the ground. Exhausted, she let out a sigh of relief. Kim's jaw was nearly on the ground. Rin rushed over and knelt down beside her.

"Hey, you OK?" she asked.

It took Kim a moment to even register she was being spoken to.

"Yeah…. yeah."

Rin grabbed her hand and pulled her up off the ground. Kim rolled her shoulder in a small circle and grabbed at her shin. She bit down on her lip fighting the pain in both. They walked over to where Charlotte was. Rin bent down next to her.

"Hey, you good?" Rin asked again.

"Yeah," Charlotte nodded, panting, "just give me a minute."

Aaliyah then walked up behind Kim and Rin with an appalled look on her face. She shifted her gaze between all three of them with impatient eyes.

"Uhhh so no one's gonna say anything?! We're not gonna talk about what just happened?! Why was that guy whoopin us like that?! And what the hell is that thing?!" Aaliyah cried pointing towards the bladed weapon.

Charlotte looked over at it. She gently ran her fingers over one of its blood-stained blades.

"It looks like…. some kinda flying guillotine chakram hybrid? The craftsmanship of it is actually pretty incredible. Never seen anything like it. I don't even know where you'd get something like this from. This is some extremely advanced weaponry."

"A flying what?!" Aaliyah cried.

Kim looked over the weapon herself and took notice of the intricate designs all about the weapon's base. There were several dragons and flowers engraved into the steel piece.

"He had full control of it, too," Kim added, "He's been using that thing for years, no amateur could've handled something like this the way he was. He didn't just get this somewhere, it was made for him."

"No amateur? This one here sure seems to know how to whip one around," Aaliyah said pointing to Charlotte.

"Look, I just threw it and pulled it back," Charlotte said pushing herself back up to a knee.

"Whatever, we're done now right?" Aaliyah asked, "We can all go back to livin our normal lives now that this creep is dead right?"

"Nope."

Kim, Aaliyah, and Charlotte all turned around and saw Rin crouched over the man's body. In her hand she held another voice recorder. She pressed play.

"Hmph…. I'd liked to be impressed but this is only the beginning. What would be the fun in hunting

those too weak to even defend themselves? The satisfaction is there, surely, but it just ain't enough. Don't worry, the next'll be twice as fun. A word of advice to all of you though, don't get caught alone."

Rin clenched the bridge of her nose and shook her head in disbelief.

"He's toyin with us, we were supposed to win," she said.

They all stood in silence for a moment as they thought.

"I mean, what's this guy's plan?" Aaliyah asked, "It sounds like he wants us alive until he's ready to see us but if he's gonna keep sending people like that...."

"We can't predict who or what's coming next," Rin said.

All three of them quickly looked to Kim in unison. "We're just gonna have to wait and watch our backs," she said.

"Wait?" Charlotte questioned.

"What else can we do right now? We can't ignore him, street thugs are one thing but now he's sending real assassins after us. Until he reveals himself and we can go directly at him, we have to play his game, there's no other option."

Distressed expressions came over all their faces. They knew she was right. As helpless and uncomfortable as it made them feel, without any real leads to go on waiting was all they could do.

"What do y'all think he meant by don't get caught alone?" Rin asked.

They all looked back and forth amongst each

other but no one uttered a response.

"I don't know but honestly I'm over this guy and his riddles," Charlotte groaned.

"We'll figure it out later. Let's not leave this body or this…. *thing* up here either," Kim said eyeing the weapon. "Let's get rid of this stuff and get back to the pool hall."

"Hey, I was thinkin about that." Aaliyah began, "If this guy's watchin us as close as we think he is, don't you think he knows we're crashin there?

"I'm sure he does," Kim said.

~

"I don't know, Lu. I heard the explosion and whoever did it was gone by the time I got outside. I put out the fire and then Rin picked me up," Kim said.

Lying to LuLu felt so wrong to her, like returning to a bad habit. She was glad their conversation was over the phone, her body language showed she didn't even believe anything she was saying.

"OK, but you didn't think to clean it up first? Both our lawns look crazy right now. When you didn't answer your phone, I got worried."

Kim used the blade of her hair pick to cut a strip of gauze and began rewrapping the cut on her arm. Between the gash and the now numbing pain in her shoulder and shin she could barely move.

"I know I know, I just…. I was in a rush. My phone was actually in the car when it blew up. I had to go buy a new car, grab this burner phone, and then I had to help Rin with something and…. I'll get someone to come clean everything up tomorrow, I promise."

LuLu let out a desperate sigh.

"You don't know who did it, like at all?"

"No, I can't even begin to imagine who or…"

"Well, there's no way it was random, they'd have torn up more than just your car."

"Yeah," Kim agreed in a hushed tone.

She pulled the gauze strip tightly around her arm and tucked under the loose end. The cut still stung a bit.

"Hey, if you talk to Cindy don't mention anything to her OK? I don't want her worrying."

Lulu sucked her teeth at her request.

"Kim, I feel like this is the kinda stuff she deserves to know about."

"I just don't wanna worry her Lu. I'm not asking you to lie, I'm just sayin don't say anything, OK?"

LuLu went mute for a few moments. Kim imagined she was either rolling her eyes, twisting her lips into a frown, or both.

"Alright Kim," she heaved, "at least call the police OK?"

Kim wouldn't dare, but she was tired of going back and forth.

"I will, I'll send someone to come clean up tomorrow. I'm stayin at Rin's tonight but I'll see you…. soon."

LuLu responded with another deep sigh. Kim

could hear it; she was both worried and frustrated.

"Alright bye," she said ending the call before Kim could reply back.

Kim placed her hand over her forehead and ran her fingers through her hair. She understood LuLu's frustration but she was twice as frustrated, and couldn't even explain to her why. It was eating at her.

She was sitting on the floor with her back pressed against the wall of the pool hall's back room. The room was empty, there were only the four walls, a squeaky wooden floor, and her inside. Rin, Aaliyah, and Charlotte were all asleep in the pool hall's main area while Kim kept watch.

She looked down at her phone and read the time, "11:07". Dropping her phone and hair pick to the floor, she buried her head in her knees. She felt hot, hotter than usual, and was sweating profusely. She felt light headed as well. Her mind kept replaying the scene on The Hill. Though it far from the most gruesome thing she had seen in her life, it struck her differently than anything else she had seen before for some reason

She reached into her pocket and pulled out a small bag of trail mix. She tore the bag open and poured a handful of salted nuts, seeds, berries, and chocolate into her hand. She threw the handful back into her mouth and rested her head back into the wall gazing up at the ceiling as she chewed.

"Knock knock," Helena smiled peeking into the room, "mind if I bother you for a bit?"

Kim didn't even bother looking at her. The throbbing pain in her head gave away who it was before she even spoke.

"You're going to regardless," she said in between chews.

"You're right," she said entering the room with a smile.

She sat down at Kim's right in the same position. Kim still hadn't brought her eyes down from the ceiling. Helena looked over at her and extended her hand out. Kim stopped chewing and turned her head towards her. The grin on Helena's face inexplicably both sickened and comforted her. She handed the bag of trail mix over to her without a word. Helena smiled as she took the bag.

"You know," Helena said, pouring some of the mix into her hand, "today was one of those days that only you could've lived. Got held at gunpoint in a grocery store, got your car blown up, bought a new super car, beheaded a man…. I mean seriously, your autobiography would sell millions K."

Helena dumped the handful of trail mix into her mouth and started chewing as she continued to speak.

"And I mean, this is just a Tuesday for you. Some people pay good money to get the kind of thrills that your life just seems to be made up of."

She poured herself another handful that she immediately threw back. The entire time she kept talking, babbling on about the day. Kim tuned her voice out though as she had keyed in on her actions instead. She realized she had never seen Helena eat anything before. She remembered seeing her sip tea years ago but never eat. While the actions weren't incredibly different from each other something about Helena munching on trail mix felt odd to watch. It made her question what she believed she knew about her.

Kim discreetly looked her up and down as she continued to chatter on. She started to wonder, with all the time that had passed since Helena disappeared four years ago, had she changed, had her existence changed? Kim's eyes fell down to her hair pick resting on the floor and a sudden impulsive thought struck her mind. She grabbed the pick, released the blade, and stuck it into Helena's arm. Helena instantly hushed, swallowed what was left in her mouth, and seemingly muddled, looked down at her arm.

Kim, looking at her arm as well, was surprised the blade appeared to be actually stuck in Helena. She wasn't sure how she was expecting it to feel but it wasn't for it to feel as though she were stabbing a real person. Kim's eyes slowly rose until she saw Helena's face. She was still staring in shock at the blade in her arm. Eventually she looked up and their eyes locked. They were both completely mute staring at each other.

"Uhhh..." Kim began.

"Ow!" Helena screamed.

She jumped hard, jerked away, and grabbed at her arm where the blade had stuck. Kim jumped back as well frightened by her sudden reaction.

"What the.... Kim?! What was that for?!" she cried.

"Wh-what?! You.... you felt that?!" Kim asked

in a hushed panic.

"*Did I feel you stab me?!* Yes?!" she replied in a bent tone.

"Wha…. wait, how? I thought you weren't real?"

"Ugh Kim?!" she huffed, "I'm real to you! I'm real in *your* mind!"

"But…. but…" Kim stuttered.

"Which means *your* mind can perceive me being hurt, if *you* hurt me!"

She quickly reached for the gauze she had cut from to wrap her own wound and tore a strip off. She pulled Helena's hand from her arm and saw blood had begun slowly spilling from the small puncture. Kim was completely thrown.

"I'm…. I'm sorry. I didn't know. Are you OK?" she asked.

Helena held an unsatisfied look on her face. She didn't appear upset, just annoyed.

"Yeah, I'll be fine. I'm actually surprised it took you this long to try somethin like that."

"Hold on," Kim began to press herself up, "we got a first aid kit in the…"

"Wh-Kim? You're gonna waste first aid equipment on your imaginary friend? Good luck explaining that one to them in the morning. Just wrap it so I don't have blood runnin down my arm."

Kim sat back down and shook her head as she began wrapping her arm.

"I-I don't know, it just didn't occur to me that you could feel pain. My brain really created something that seems so real it can literally bleed, it's

156

kinda trippy."

"After all this time that's just now freakin you out?"

"I don't know, my mind is all over the place right now. You sure you're OK?"

"Yeah, I'm fine but could you not do that again?"

"Yeah.... sorry," she said finishing the wrap.

"What's up with you? You seem more on edge than you normally are. Did watchin that dude's head roll on The Hill really mess you up that bad?" Helena asked.

"It's not just that, this whole situation. Life was so good and then.... all this. I mean look where I am. Literally the one place on earth I never wanted to step foot back inside of. And this guy hunting us for whatever reason, leaving all these cryptic messages. I just wanna live the rest of my life. Is that so wrong?"

"Why would that be wrong?" Helena asked.

"Maybe I just don't deserve anything I want anymore. I've done so much terrible stuff in my life maybe I don't deserve..."

"Kim, it's not wrong to want anything, desire is not a sin. Actually, desire is an essential trait of all living things. Without desire, without a want for anything ever, what would you even do day to day? Think about it, hunger is a desire for sustenance, boredom is a desire for stimulation, fear is a desire for survival. Every thought or emotion translated into action is the reaction to a desire for something. If you didn't want, if you didn't desire anything, you'd be the equivalent to a zombie walking around every day.

So, I don't wanna hear any more about you not deserving to live the rest of your life because of your past. It's your past, but you moved past it. Unfortunately, others haven't and because it's still your past and you own it, that's something you gotta deal with, but you still deserve what you want, especially if all you want is something as simple as to live life. Everyone deserves at least a little bit of what they want, you're no exception."

Kim thought for a moment. Again, she couldn't say Helena was right, but nothing she said struck her as evidently wrong either.

"So then what do you want?" Kim asked, "You never told me, what do you desire?"

Helena's serious tone quickly turned giddy from Kim's question. She seemed excited to answer.

"Like I said, desire is an essential trait of all living things but remember, I'm not actually living. Your mind allows you to see me in what appears to be a human form, but I'm not really human. I'm closer to that of a spirit than human really. My sole existence is to help you.… I think anyway. I don't know much else to be honest. But existing outside your mind for the time I have as well as drawing on the memories and experiences that our connection grants me access to I've been able to view the world through both your eyes and my own. Maybe I'm just cursed and ended up being the offset of the unluckiest person on the face of the earth, but truthfully Kim, after what I've seen from your life I don't wanna be human, and so I don't particularly even want to experience desire the way you humans do. Y'all deal with too much garbage on a regular basis and then just chalk it up as life, or at least you do anyway. I couldn't live like that."

"OK so, you don't have desires then? Cause the other day you said…"

"That we're of the same mind and so why wouldn't I? Here's the thing K, I don't have desires, I have one, singular, and it's what I believe to be my only purpose for existing, helping you. Now whatever I need to do or obtain in the process, I guess you could argue that becomes a desire of mine as well, sure, but in reality, I exist only to your mind as a tool for helping mend it, and so that's my only desire. I don't know anything else."

"So helping?" Kim asked.

"Helping *you* Kim. I can't help anyone else, I don't exist to anyone else."

"But what if you couldn't help me?"

"What do you mean?"

"Four years ago when you disappeared, you disappeared because I was happy and so you couldn't help me anymore at that point. But you showed something that looked like grief that last night we sat at my kitchen table and talked. If fear is a desire, wouldn't grief be one too?"

"Yes, a desire to be happy."

"So, you desired to be happy then, right?"

Helena shrugged, "Hmmm…. I guess."

Kim thought for a moment, "That sadness you showed that night, was it because you knew what your fate would be after you disappeared or because you didn't?"

"A little of both," Helena said.

"But you don't know what it was now, you don't know what or where you were until you popped back up in front of me the other night?"

"It's a strange existence I have huh?" Helena smirked.

"OK, let me start over." Kim said scratching her head, "Never mind helping me, if you and I's connection was somehow severed tomorrow but you continued to exist and your fate was in your own hands, what would you wanna do?"

Helena's eyes grew wide from her question. The grin on her face told she was even a bit impressed by it. She placed her hands behind her head, leaned back into the wall, and stared up at the ceiling as she thought hard.

"That's deep K. Unfortunately, the only answer I can give you isn't. Again, I only really know what I was created to do, help you. And so, if it couldn't be you, and you'd always be my first, second, and third choice, I guess I'd just wanna help the next person that needed me. It's the only thing I know how to do. Sorry, I know it's not much but that's all I got."

Kim was intrigued by her answer. The way Helena described herself was comparable to that of a machine that knows to do nothing else other than what it was programmed to do. But her conscious decision to want to help another if she was unable to help who she was meant to, Kim thought unprogrammable. She didn't believe anything could've put that answer in her but Helena herself.

"It's enough," Kim said.

Two soft knocks against the doorframe took Kim's attention from Helena. Aaliyah stood in the doorway.

"Hey, you wanna sleep? I can take over till morning."

"Yeah, thanks," Kim said pushing herself up.

"You alright?" she asked.

Kim froze against the wall before making it onto her feet.

"Yeah, why?"

Aaliyah shrugged, "You been kinda quiet since this afternoon."

Kim exhaled and slowly slid back down to the floor; she knew a talk was coming. Helena stood and quietly exited the room. Aaliyah didn't give her even the slightest of looks as she passed by her. Any further doubt of Helena's existence to others immediately went out the window.

Aaliyah walked over and sat down next to Kim. She took a deep breath and shook her head before speaking.

"Today was..."

"Crazy?" Kim offered finishing her thought.

"Yeah, that and a few other things."

Aaliyah looked around the empty room and frowned.

"You ever think you'd end up back inside this place?" she asked.

"The only thing I prayed for the last four years was that I wouldn't."

"One decision, we're here because of one

decision. Because we said yes," Aaliyah bit her lip in shame.

It was a thought that had plagued Kim for years. How different her life could've been had she just said no to The Pool.

"Why'd you say yes?" Kim asked her.

The face she made in response led Kim to believe bitter memories were the reason.

"When I graduated high school, college wasn't really an option, my parents barely had the money to put me and my sister through grade school. So, I started runnin the streets. Dealin here and there, but mostly robbin and lootin just to eat. In the two or whatever years I was doin it I only got caught once. Broke into Terrance's house one night, thought I had scored, got some jewelry, some cash, all that. But I got greedy. I knew I didn't get everything I could've so I doubled back the next night. Thought I'd got him again. Climbed out the window I came in and as soon as I turned around he had a pistol pointed right between my eyes."

Kim's stomach dropped.

"He asked me why and I told him I was just tryin to eat. He invited me in, fed me, and then showed me the footage his security cameras caught. My face was completely exposed in it. He gave me a choice, he said he'd let me go and keep everything I stole but he'd turn the footage over to the police, or he'd erase the tapes and let me keep half of what I took if I agreed to help him with somethin in the morning. I took the second option. I was terrified though. Couldn't imagine what he wanted from me but I figured the worst. That next morning, he brought me here and introduced me to you."

Kim vaguely remembered the day Terrance introduced them. She remembered seeing Aaliyah for the first time and believing she wouldn't last a day as an assassin.

"Livin out my car was gettin old, the streets were gettin old. At that point I had already given up on my life to be honest, so when he told me he had fifteen grand for me to gun down some guy, I took it."

Aaliyah's story only surprised Kim because it was the first time she had heard it. It sounded like a typical life story from someone who lived in Joy City.

"Why'd you say yes? I mean, I know about your foster parents and all but was that it?" Aaliyah asked.

"Basically," Kim nodded, "For some reason, I thought I was doin the right thing."

"And Terrance let you think that?"

"I guess…"

Aaliyah sucked her teeth.

"You know…. I love him, I swear I do, he basically saved my life, but god he took advantage of us bein young and dumb. He sat back and co-signed us literally throwing our lives away."

She was right. Terrance introduced them both to The Pool when they were spiraling, emotionally vulnerable, when things were so bad in their lives they were liable to say yes to anything. She began to wonder what Pedro and Charlotte's stories were.

163

"Yeah, at least he had the mind to stop when things got bad all those years ago," Kim said.

Aaliyah looked at her bent for a moment.

"He wasn't going to though."

"What do you mean?" Kim asked cutting her eyes.

Aaliyah's expression turned blank. She was surprised Kim didn't seem to know what she was speaking of.

"That night, Christmas, when Rin first showed up and things spiraled out of control, he wasn't gonna dead The Pool. He spent the week after trying to figure out how we were gonna keep operating after bein exposed. Me and Charlotte had to talk him out of it."

Kim's mouth fell open a bit.

"I mean, I doubt it was because he wanted to but more so because it was all he knew. He and your parents started The Pool fresh outta their teens. That night after you and Rin left, I asked him, you say you love us right, you say you love us like your own right? Well, you just lost one of us, you ready to lose another? I told him it won't be me, I told him I was done, I was walkin either way. Charlotte said the same."

Aaliyah relaxed back into the wall and shook her head. It was as if she were dreading just retelling the events.

"This life we all chose to step into, we all knew it was wrong from the jump, but we all still stepped into it anyway. And by some miracle me, you, Charlotte, and Terrance made it out with our lives,

164

millions of dollars richer too, but it could've went another way. That night I told him I was done and that he needed to be done too. I told him we gotta stop, all of us, we gotta stop this, before it stops us."

Kim couldn't speak, a lump had formed in her throat. Her entire body went stiff. She felt like she was about to cry, but didn't actually know what she would've even been crying about. Aaliyah noticed how spooked she looked and immediately knew to stop talking. She placed her hand on Kim's leg and gently patted it.

"Go get some sleep, I'll watch till morning."

Chapter 6

Two of a Kind II

"I don't even know really, the last place I remember having it was at the store. Maybe it slipped out my pocket or somethin," Kim said.

"How does a whole cell phone just slip out your pocket without you noticing?" Cindy asked.

"I don't know but I couldn't find it anywhere so for now just save me under this number."

"Alright."

Kim rolled her shoulder and winced from the pain.

"You get your finals scores back yet?" she asked attempting to mask her grunts.

"Not yet, probably Friday at the earliest."

"When are you helping Lei-Ling move into her apartment?"

"Tomorrow hopefully. If so, I can clean the dorm and probably be home by the weekend."

Kim's stomach dropped.

"Uhhh…. well, don't worry about rushin back. Ummm…. I told Ms. C I'd be up at The Home all this week. Hate for you to come back and me not even be able to spend much time with you."

"It's no big deal, after these finals all I wanna do is sleep anyway. I won't be offended if you're not there. I actually talked to Ms. C yesterday and she said I'm always welcome to come back and help out up there if I'm ever free so..."

Kim silently cursed herself for spewing out yet another weak lie.

"Well, just let me know sweetheart," she said.

"I will. Ummm…. hey, did you talk to Aunt Rin about what we talked about Monday?"

The topic Kim was hoping to avoid. She wished she could've just hung up and pretended like the question hadn't been asked.

"Not yet, she's been runnin around a lot and everything's just been really crazy since she lost her job so we haven't had time to sit down together. But I promise I'll bring it up to her soon."

Kim wasn't sure if that sentence were a complete lie or if some parts of it were even partially true. She suddenly recalled how awful and conflicted it was to be a pathological liar.

"OK…. well, have you been thinkin about it at all?" she asked.

Kim sighed heavily before answering.

"Ummm…. yeah, I think…. I think you're right. This city is gettin old, or has gotten old rather, and it's probably time to consider a move. Once I talk to Aunt Rin I'll let you know."

Kim heard Cindy let out a sigh of relief. If only she knew the truth behind her consideration.

"Cool," she said.

Kim could hear in her voice how pleased she was with her answer.

"Well, we're about to go get something to eat. I'll call you later though."

"OK baby, be safe…. I mean, have fun," she corrected, "enjoy yourself."

"I will, love you."

"Love you, too."

The phone hung up and Kim dropped it onto the wooden floor beneath her. She blew air out her nose in frustration and looked up at the ceiling. She felt like she was spiraling again, a familiar yet unwelcomed state.

Sitting with her back to the wall of the pool hall's main area, with only herself and the small kerosene lantern by her side, she watched shadows rise and fall from the lantern's dancing flame. She found the ever-shifting amber light against the dark colored wood so calming, so relaxing. It helped sooth the massive headache she was suffering from.

"What's all this huffin and puffin about missy?"

Kim dropped her head down and cut her eyes at Helena smiling sitting crisscrossed in front of her. She felt like her head was going to explode, so she let it sink down until she was staring at the floor.

Helena's smile faded. "Hey, what's wrong?" she asked.

Kim remained mute and still.

"Hey?" Helena moaned, pushing on her knee, "Talk to me, what's wrong?"

"I'm stressed out Helena," Kim snapped at her.

Helena drew back a bit and twisted her face at her response.

"Stressed out? How? About what?"

Kim lifted her head and shot an irked expression back at her.

"Really?" she asked, "Have you not seen what I've went through these past few days?"

Helena rolled her eyes at her. She shook her head like a parent disappointed in their child.

"I guess it's not your fault," she sighed.

Kim looked up at her confused.

"What isn't?" Kim asked.

"That you're so susceptible to stress, that it always breaks you down so easily."

Kim cut her eyes at her again unsure of the angle she was taking.

"So who's fault is it then?"

"Your foster parents really," Helena shrugged, "they failed you."

Kim's expression quickly turned, offended by Helena's claim.

"Excuse me?"

"Calm down, I'm not tryin to attack your folks but, really it is their fault."

"How?"

Helena took a deep breath, looked directly into Kim's eyes, and began to speak.

"When you were younger, at some point your foster parents sat you down and talked to you about certain things, right? Gave you advice here and there, right? Whether it be manners, responsibility, dealing with the opposite sex, drugs and alcohol, etcetera etcetera. These talks were had so that they could pass along their knowledge to you in hopes of helping you navigate through life as smoothly as possible. But let me ask you something, of all those talks, all the times they sat you down in an effort to teach you something.... did they ever sit you down and teach you how to deal with stress? Did Terrance? Ms. C? Anyone?"

The answer was no, but Kim kept mute because she knew she wasn't done, she hadn't talked long enough yet.

Helena took another deep breath before continuing.

"But really, it's not even their faults, they couldn't have taught you how because really, they didn't know either. Because just like they all failed to teach you, their parents failed to teach them. It's a lesson that's almost always forgotten by parents and guardians, yet stress is linked to most major causes of death. See, what happens is parents fail to teach their children how to deal with stress but will allow themselves to be seen dealing with stress in various ways in front of their young, impressionable children. This is where people pick up their bad stress habits. Stress eating, stress drinking, ranting and raving, pouting. When you don't know how to deal with something in life you naturally look back to your childhood and how you saw your authoritative figures deal with it, and, unfortunately when it comes to stress, rarely does a child ever have an intelligent and effective demonstration to look back to. That's why stress gets to you, why it gets to most people, because you weren't taught any better. But that's not your fault."

Kim couldn't tell if it was the confidence with which she spoke or if Helena was truly just brilliant when she wasn't clowning around and making jokes. When Helena spoke seriously, she articulated words better than anyone Kim knew. She couldn't help but listen and ask questions.

"Then how? What's the intelligent and effective way of dealing with stress?"

Helena adjusted her beanie and crossed her arms in front of her chest.

"A dictionary defines stress as a state of mental and emotional strain or tension resulting from adverse or very demanding circumstances. Now, notice the first part of the definition states that stress is a mental and emotional state. Unless you are deemed mentally insane or unstable by someone qualified to deem you as such you are always in control of anything having to do with your mentality as well as your emotions. At times hardship can make it feel as though your emotions are overpowering you. But realistically, so long as you are still in your right mind, which…. you know…. you kinda are, there is never a time in which your emotions are in control of you. All of this meaning these adverse or very demanding circumstances are not really what's causing you stress, you, yourself, are causing you stress. We can come to this conclusion because, again, as the definition states, stress is a mental and emotional state, both of which you are in control of at all times."

"OK, but how…"

"Hold on, I'm getting there." Helena hushed her, "The second half of the definition says that stress comes following adverse or demanding circumstances. You of all people know life is full of those. There is no way around life's adversity. Bad things, or at least things that test you in ways, are going to happen, that's a promise. Knowing this, you should never fear anything. You may not know what's gonna happen but you know eventually something will, so when it does, rather than focus on the fact that it's arrived, focus on moving through it, moving past it. Kim, the secret to beating stress lies within the answer to this simple question. What does stress do for you?"

"*What does it do for you?*" Kim repeated.

"Does it ease the adversity of the situation? Does it make the circumstances any less demanding? Does it cause the hardship to go away? Does it speed up the healing process of whatever hurt the happening causes? Does it even make you feel any better? No. In fact, it only makes you feel worse about the already bad thing. You could conjure up a million different hypothetical situations and I guarantee you, you cannot come up with a single case in which stressing over the situation makes anything any better."

"I mean, I get what you're saying but I don't think it's that simple."

Helena raised an eyebrow at her claim.

"Is it not? Let's say your rent is due. You need

to have a hundred dollars by the first of the month. It's currently eleven p.m. on the thirty-first and you only have ninety-eight. Wait an hour and see if stress lends you that two dollars."

"Yeah, but…" Kim began.

"Let's say you got a test tomorrow you have to study for. You have a bunch of material to look at and it's overwhelming you and you just can't deal. You got two options, stress over it all night or study. Regardless of which option you choose, the teacher's still gonna hand you a test tomorrow and you're still gonna be expected to pass it. One of those options will at least give you a fighter's chance at passing though, the other will just make you feel worse about not knowing the material."

"OK…. but…"

"Let's say work is gettin to you. You got that one annoying co-worker always fake smilin in your face, talkin about you behind your back. Your supervisor is always in your ear about somethin, always tryin to tell you what you're doin wrong. And your boss has you feelin like the paycheck you work for every week just isn't enough to justify havin to hear their mouth every day. You can sit there at your little cubicle and stress about it all day long or you can start lookin for a new job, start your own business, or find yourself any other way out. Either way stress didn't have your back in the first example and you still owe your landlord two dollars, so you better figure it out quick."

"OK OK, I get it," Kim said.

"Kim, all stress does is bring you down more.

All you're doing is harping on one of those promised adverse or demanding circumstances that the definition of stress mentions. It's bad enough you have to go through whatever it is but you're now gonna force yourself to think about it to the point that you begin making yourself feel worse about it with absolutely no chance of those thoughts doing anything positive for you? Just think about that for a second, is that not completely insane?"

"OK, so what's the correct way to deal with it then? I get it, you're a profound speaker, but you haven't answered my question. How do you battle stress effectively?"

Helena shook her head.

"You don't battle it Kim, you beat it. Remember this, you can't be defeated in a battle you're not in. Adopt the mindset that stress is not real, it's something your mind creates as a response to things it doesn't find pleasant. But unpleasantries are just another part of life, you know that. So, when you're faced with adversity, rather than stress over it, focus on moving through it, moving past it, moving over it, moving around it. Whenever you feel it creeping back into your mind stop and ask yourself, what is this stress gonna do for me? I promise you the answer will never be anything positive. Cast it out Kim. Your mind is already primed to being trained, it's been trained for years, control it. Don't allow it to manifest stress within you."

She was speaking in a tone Kim remembered rarely hearing from her. There was no joy, no giggles following every word, no batting of her eyes, she was preaching to her. As she listened, she couldn't find a single point to disagree or debate. She hated that.

Helena took another breath and softened her tone a bit.

"The short answer, stress isn't real, it's a figment of your imagination that only exists within your mind if you allow it to."

She leaned forward a bit and looked deep into Kim's eyes.

"Don't allow it to," she added.

"Kim?! You up?!" Rin called from outside.

Helena eyed in the direction of the pool hall's main entrance and smiled. Kim took this as the benediction to her lecture. She slowly rose to her feet and stepped around the corner to see Rin poking her head through the blue tarp leading outside.

"What's up?" Kim asked.

"Come out here for a sec," she said nodding outside.

Kim looked back to where Helena was sitting and noticed she was gone. She twisted her lips and headed outside.

It was dark, the sun had already set. After the events of the previous day they all decided to stay inside the pool hall for the day to rest. Currently, it seemed to be the only safe place for them. Aaliyah and Charlotte were standing out a few feet from the pool hall talking. Kim drew both of their eyes as she and Rin walked over to them.

"How's Cindy?" Aaliyah asked.

"Better than us," Kim smirked, "what's up?"

"Tryin to figure out our next move," Charlotte

said.

"Arming ourselves would be a good start," Kim said.

"I got some family that's for sure packin somethin, I could give them a call?" Aaliyah suggested.

"You wanna risk getting them involved though?" Kim asked.

".... Nah," Aaliyah said.

"Well, we're runnin outta options," Charlotte said, "eventually we're probably gonna have to go to someone. There's no special weapons delivery service out here, we gotta consider something eventually."

Her point was valid. They needed something to protect themselves, likely sooner than later.

"Maybe we could…"

Kim's sentence stopped short as her stomach loudly growled drawing all their attention.

"Was that you?" Rin asked her.

Kim nodded.

"I'm starving too really, and I'm sick of chips and trail mix," Aaliyah said.

"Yeah, something heavier would be nice." Kim added.

"What do y'all want?" Rin asked them.

"Anything, just something," Aaliyah groaned.

"We can get some fast food somewhere, just something we can grab and get back with quick," Charlotte said.

"Maybe y'all should stay here," Kim said to them.

"Geez Kim, what you don't want us ridin in your new car? We've had just as many showers as you this week," Aaliyah teased.

Kim sucked her teeth.

"It's not that, this place seems to be the only safe spot we have in the city right now. I'll go by myself just to keep…"

"No, no way," Rin said turning towards her, "If this pool hall is the only safe place we have right now you're definitely not goin out alone. That creep on the recording literally just yesterday warned us not to be caught alone, whatever that means."

"I'll be fine Rin," Kim assured her.

"Yeah, you will cause I'm goin with you. You're not goin out there by yourself, especially not with that shoulder."

"How's your shoulder feelin by the way?" Charlotte asked gently massaging it.

Kim clinched her teeth hard, it hurt to the touch.

"It's fine, just a little sore," she said.

"And the cut?" Charlotte asked rubbing over her bandages, "You clean it today?"

"Yeah, it's fine," Kim said flexing her hand.

"Alright let's get goin, it's already dark out." Rin said.

"Just grab me a salad or something," Aaliyah said.

"Same," Charlotte echoed.

"Let me grab my keys," Kim said.

~

"Here you go, have a nice night, ma'am," a redheaded girl smiled from the drive-thru window as she handed a large plastic bag down to Kim.

"Thank you, you too," Kim said passing the bag to Rin sitting in the passenger's seat. "Make sure everything's in there before I pull off."

Rin began looking through the bag ensuring everything was inside.

"Hey?" the girl from the window called.

Kim turned back around to face her.

"I love your car," she smiled.

Kim was a bit thrown off having already forgotten she was sitting inside a hundred-thousand dollar vehicle.

"Oh…. uhhh…. thank you," she awkwardly smiled back.

"I've never seen one in person, surprised to see one in Joy City at all," she said.

"Yeah…. ummm actually…"

"We don't live here," Rin interrupted with a smile, "just passing through."

Kim looked and noticed the discreet hard stare she was giving her.

"Yeah, just passing through," Kim echoed.

"Oh, OK," the girl nodded, "well, y'all have a good night."

"You too," Rin smiled back.

Kim rolled up her window and began driving off. She looked over to Rin with a curious stare.

"Look, I don't trust anyone right now," Rin shrugged, "the least amount of human interaction we have the better. I'm sorry but this car was a bad idea, draws way too much attention and that's the last thing we need right now."

"I know but on short notice it was the only thing I could get with no papers on it. Trust me, I went there lookin for a beater."

Kim glanced down at the dashboard and noticed the car was near empty on gas.

"Ugh…. need to fill up before we head back," she groaned.

"Fill up? You bought this car yesterday, it's already on E?"

"I bought it illegally, you don't get a free fill up with that."

Rin rolled her eyes, "Gas station right across the street."

"I see it."

Kim crossed the street and pulled into the small lot. It was mostly empty. Only two other cars sat out front. She pulled up next to one of the pumps and parked.

"I'mma grab some more bottled water since we're here, I think we're almost out," Rin said.

Kim reached in her pocket and pulled out a few bills and handed them to Rin.

"Here, put thirty on gas and get whatever else you can with the rest."

"Alright," Rin nodded.

They both exited the car. As Kim began walking around to the car's gas tank she stepped in something that stuck to the bottom of her shoe. She tried to scrape it off but couldn't. She lifted her foot and turned the bottom of her shoe up to see she had stepped in a massive wad of bubble gum.

"Ugh…. really?" she sucked her teeth.

She grabbed the gum with her bare hands and pulled at it. It was stringy and wet from what she could only hope was just saliva.

"Ewww, Kim, you don't know whose mouth that's been in," Rin cried scrunching her face up.

"Well I gotta get it off," she said pulling the last bit from her shoe before flinging it into a nearby trash can.

"Come wash your hands before you catch somethin," Rin said.

"Yeah," Kim said frowning at her wet finger tips.

They both walked into the gas station and were greeted with a slight nod from an old man sitting behind the counter. Kim looked up and saw a long rectangular restroom sign above a door tucked around a corner.

"Go ahead and pay for everything. I'll be back," Kim said.

She walked around the corner and into the bathroom. She turned the water as hot as it could go and used an excessive amount of hand soap as she scrubbed each of her fingers. After a full minute of scrubbing, she turned off the water and used a few paper towels to dry her hands off. Before she turned around to leave, she looked in the mirror and stared at herself. There were bags under her eyes from her lack of sleep, her hair was a complete mess, and her skin looked dry and dehydrated. She closed her eyes and took a deep breath.

Stress isn't real.

It's just a figment of your imagination.

It can only exist within your mind if you allow it to.

Don't allow it to.

She whispered the words to herself, with hope that reciting them regularly she would eventually find them to be as true as she was told they were. She opened her eyes, took one last look at herself in the mirror, and turned around.

As she pushed on the door she squinted and quietly hissed from the pain in her shoulder. Before she could fully open her eyes, she felt a hand grab at her arm and jerk her sideways. She gasped and froze seeing Rin with her index finger pressed up against her lips.

"Shhh..." she hushed her.

Her back was pressed against the wall as if she were hiding from something.

"What?" Kim asked in a whisper.

Rin thumbed around the corner motioning for her to listen. Kim leaned against the wall.

"They just walked in here, two women, a set of twins," a raspy feminine voice said.

"I-I don't..."

"Don't try to hide them, you don't wanna get tangled up in this," another lighter female voice said.

Kim looked at Rin puzzled.

"They walked in and started pressin him about us," Rin whispered.

"Did they see you?" Kim asked.

"Nah, I ducked down before they could."

"They armed?"

"Not sure."

They both turned their attention back towards the two women interrogating the clerk.

"You got five seconds old man," the lighter voice warned.

Rin looked to Kim waiting for her to move. Kim pressed her lips together and pushed past Rin stepping out from around the corner.

"Hey?!" she called out.

The two women quickly spun around. They wore hoods and masks that left only a bit of their faces exposed around their eyes. One was black with a deep ebony skin tone. The other, a bit shorter in height, had a more peach colored complexion.

"Leave him alone, you want us right?" Kim asked pulling Rin from around the corner.

The four of them had a brief stare down until the lighter skinned woman reached at her side and flung a throwing blade towards them. Kim leaned out the way and the blade stuck into the wall next to her.

"OK, well they're definitely armed," Rin said.

The woman then charged at them. Kim grabbed the long shelf full of chips, cakes, and candies next to them and pulled it down onto the woman stopping her advance.

"C'mon!" Kim said as she darted for the exit.

"Wh-wait, we're running?!" Rin asked.

"C'mon!" Kim barked again over her shoulder.

Before she could move the woman had tossed the shelf aside. She threw another blade that tagged

Rin's right ankle. She shrieked and immediately fell to a knee. Kim stopped and turned around.

"Rin!" she called to her.

She was then blindsided by the other woman who had speared her from the side. They both went crashing through the store window onto the curb outside. Kim landed on her back with the woman on top of her. She wallowed in pain for only a second before she punched the woman in her face and kicked her off.

Rin and the other woman then burst through the other window wrestling with each other on foot. Rin was pushed back until her foot missed the curb and she fell backwards with the woman landing on top of her. Kim jumped up, ran over, kicked the woman in her side, and threw her off. She quickly pulled Rin to her feet.

"You OK?! Can you run?!" Kim asked looking her up and down.

"Yeah yeah, I'm good," she nodded.

"Alright c'mon!" Kim said pulling her along.

They circled around the side of the building. Kim spotted a dumpster pushed up against a wooden fence.

"Up the dumpster, over the fence, hurry!" Kim commanded.

Rin moved gingerly on her right ankle but eventually got up and over with Kim's help. Kim glanced back and saw the two women sprinting towards them. She quickly boosted herself up onto the dumpster and cleared the fence. She dropped down into a dark narrow alley.

"Which way?" Rin asked.

Kim looked both left and right before eventually breaking left. Rin followed closely behind her. As they ran down the alley they hopped over piles of junk in their path and sidestepped a few dumpsters and stacked crates. They stopped when they came to the end of the alley that led to a large open area. Tall apartment buildings stood on each side closing the area in.

"Dead end," Kim growled under her breath.

"OK, so, now what?" Rin asked.

The two women emerged from the alley and stopped. Kim widened her stance, ready to defend herself. Rin did the same. The two women began slowly walking to their right. Kim and Rin matched their movements step for step moving right as well to maintain the space between them. The look in their eyes was sinister. She could only imagine the wicked smiles underneath their masks.

"Keep your guard up," she whispered to Rin tucking her chain into her shirt, "they're lookin for more than a fight."

"Late night brawl in a dark alley, brings back memories, huh?" Rin said tucking her chain as well.

Kim frowned at her ill-timed humor.

"Hey!" Kim shouted towards the two women, "we don't have to do this, just tell us where we can find the person who sent you and we'll settle this with them!"

"You misunderstand," the fair-skinned woman pulled a short sword from her back and pointed it at Rin, "we *want* to do this."

The other woman then pulled a sickle from her back and glared at Kim.

"A sickle?" Rin whispered puzzled, "Where are they gettin this stuff?"

The woman wielding the short sword let out a loud cry as she began rushing towards Rin. The other charged at Kim in the same manner. Kim and Rin quickly split from each other's sides.

The sword-wielding woman threw a heavy right hook at Rin that just barely missed her face. Rin then locked her arm under hers and pulled her in close. They looked deep into each other's eyes for a moment. The woman then raised her sword and jabbed at Rin. She twisted her body sideways avoiding the stab and punched her in the mouth. She pulled her arm free and stumbled back a few steps.

Stopping just a few feet from Kim the other woman swung the sickle twice at her. Kim evaded both swings and grabbed the woman's wrist after the second miss. She twisted it and kicked her in her stomach sending her stumbling backwards. She quickly looked over towards Rin. Their eyes met briefly before they turned their focus back to their attackers.

Rin broke to her right towards the corner, the sword-wielding woman immediately chased after her.

"Watch it, she's on you!" Kim yelled to her.

The woman again charged Kim swinging the sickle at her, this time in a downward motion. It whiffed but she quickly followed it up with a kick to Kim's thigh. Kim raised her knee attempting to absorb the blow but she felt the blunt of it. Another wild swing of the sickle followed but Kim again evaded and grabbed her wrist. Before she could make a move the woman threw a punch with her free hand that Kim wiped away. The woman stayed on the offensive and delivered a rising knee that caught Kim in the stomach causing her to hunch over. She then swung the sickle down at Kim's back and its sharp tip pierced her right under her shoulder blade. As soon as she felt it touch, she immediately twisted and spun around putting space in between herself and the woman.

Kim tensed up from the pain of the small puncture. It didn't feel like anything too serious but the sting was enough for her to surmise she didn't want to get touched by it again. They fell into another brief stare down. Kim could tell from her eyes she was grinning behind her mask.

Rin had beat the woman to the corner and tore a long-rusted pipe from the side of the building. She turned around as the woman was already in the middle of a sideways slash. Rin blocked it holding the pipe vertical out in front of her and delivered a gut punch and elbow to the woman's face. She stumbled back grabbing at her jaw and hissed. Rin kept her stance. The woman let out another cry before charging again. Once she closed the space she swung the blade three times, each time missing by more than the previous swing. Rin ducked the last and rose up, grabbing the woman's arm and shoulder from behind. She placed one foot down firmly on the ground and with the other swept at the woman's feet throwing her down hard.

Rin's eyes then rose to see Kim and the other woman still trading blows with each other. The woman she had dropped then pushed herself up on her elbow and slashed upwards at Rin. She didn't react quick enough and the sword caught her forearm leaving a small laceration that began to bleed. Rin cursed aloud grabbing at her arm. She looked down at the woman with fire in her eyes. The woman swung again, this time at Rin's leg, but she lifted her foot up just in time to avoid it and came down hard, stomping on the woman's ankle. She let out a dreadful cry of pain that echoed off the brick walls surrounding them, dropping the sword onto the ground as she cried. Her scream was so loud Kim and the other woman ceased their scuffle to look and see what had happened.

"Come here," Rin growled as she grabbed the woman up from the ground.

Yanking her up by the neck of her jacket with one hand, Rin picked up the sword she had dropped with the other. She spun the woman around and held her like a hostage with the blade of the sword pressed up against her neck. The woman held a look of absolute terror in her eyes as Rin held her. Both Kim and the other woman stood frozen, gazing awestruck at Rin.

"Lynn?!" the woman cried out.

Her call snapped Kim's attention from Rin back to her. Kim grabbed her arm and bent it backwards at the joint causing her to drop her sickle. Kim pulled her hair pick from her waist and restrained the woman in the same fashion Rin had the other. She pressed the pick's blade firmly up against her neck.

Kim and Rin made eye contact but said nothing. Rin still had a furious look on her face that Kim had never seen on her before. Rin then gave her a slight nod; Kim gave her a raise of her eyebrows in return. Before she had time to wonder what the nod was supposed to mean, Rin zipped the sword across the woman's neck and let her body drop to the ground. Kim gasped and a knot formed in her stomach.

"Lynn!" the other woman screamed in horror.

Her shriek was bone chilling. Rin's eyes grew two times in size. She froze in place, unable to even blink. She herself couldn't even believe what she had done.

"Lynn! No!" the woman wailed behind her tears.

She fought hard against Kim's hold but couldn't break free from her grasp. Kim beamed at Rin until she eventually broke from her daze and their eyes met. There was fear and sorrow in her stare, she was just as surprised as they were. Rin's eyes slowly fell back down to the body lying at her feet. She looked broken, almost driven to tears herself. Then Kim noticed her eyes focus on something. She bent over the woman's body and began sifting through one of the pockets on her side.

"Get away from her you monster!" the other woman sobbed still wildly jerking about.

Rin slowly stood holding another voice recorder in her hand. She met Kim's eyes once again.

Kim began looking the woman she was holding up and down. She saw she had several pockets all over her clothes. She tucked her pick back at her side and began frisking her, going through every pocket. The woman continued to squirm, fighting against every move Kim made.

"Hey, quit it! Stay still!" Kim commanded her as they struggled against each other.

Kim eventually found a pouch on her side that had another voice recorder tucked inside. She held it up for Rin to see.

"Let me go! Someone can save her!" the woman whaled.

Kim looked over to the body and then up to Rin. She still held a hopelessly guilty look on her face. Somehow the shame of the act had managed to creep its way into Kim's mind as well as if she had committed the act. The woman's sobs only made the moment worse.

"Go! Take her and get outta here!" Kim growled kicking the woman forward.

She stumbled and fell to her knees. She crawled over to her partner and gently picked her up. She slung her limp body over her shoulder and carried her away as tears ran down her face. Kim found herself conflicted as she watched her retreat from them. She felt silly having compassion for someone who just moments earlier posed such a threat to her own life.

Rin watched in silence as the pair disappeared back into the alley. As she turned back to Kim, she shivered. She tucked the short sword under her arm and began slowly approaching Kim with an expression that pled guilty.

"Sorry…. I-I don't…"

"It's fine," Kim said cutting her apology.

She looked down at the voice recorder in her hand and looked back up at Rin. She took a deep breath and pressed the play button. The screen lit up blue but immediately fell back dim; no sound came from it. Kim pressed the button again and again it did the same. She looked up at Rin confused.

"Is it dead or something?" Rin asked.

"I mean it's still lighting up," Kim said looking it over.

Rin pressed the play button on the one she was holding and it did the same. Rin pressed the button again but the device remained silent. Kim looked back down at the one in her hand and flipped it over. She noticed several deep engravings on the back of the device. Looking closer she saw the engravings were a series of numbers and letters.

"What?" Rin asked noticing her focus.

"There's something scratched on the back."

Rin took a peek before flipping over the one she was holding.

"This one too," she said showing Kim.

Kim took it from her and held the two up next to each other. She examined them both closely and noticed one had a large letter N preceded by several numbers while the other had a large W preceded by more numbers.

"Is it a code or somethin?" Rin asked.

"No, it's a map, these are coordinates."

"Coordinates? To where?" Rin asked.

Kim stuffed both recorders down into her pockets and then bent over to pick up the sickle the woman had dropped. She tucked it halfway into the back of her pants and pulled her jacket down over what was left sticking out.

"We'll find out," she said walking back towards the mouth of the alley.

Rin used her sleeve to wipe the sword's blade clean of blood, tucked it into the back of her pants and followed behind her.

Chapter 7

Happy Birthday

Kim yawned wide and twisted her neck left and right until it cracked. She then used the palm of her hand to rub her eyes before returning it back to the steering wheel in front of her. She wasn't actually tired, she couldn't fall asleep if she wanted to, yet her body felt nearly depleted of all energy needed to function. She was bruised emotionally, physically, and mentally. She thought about Cindy's plea from earlier in the week and cursed herself for not having the mind to make the move years ago.

"You OK? I can take over," Rin said softly from the passenger seat.

Kim glanced over and shook her head.

"I'm alright," she whispered back.

Kim looked into the rearview mirror and saw both Aaliyah and Charlotte sound asleep in the backseat.

"Knocked, both of them," Rin chuckled.

"I don't blame them," Kim said.

They were driving down a desert highway. It was almost midnight and they were the only car on what seemed to be a never ending straight road. They had punched the coordinates on the back of the voice recorders into a GPS and started following a route that led into the desert plains just outside of Joy City. They had been driving for a while, seeing nothing but the road in front of them, an occasional cactus or two, and some mountain ranges off in the distance.

"How much further?" Kim asked.

Rin looked down at her cell phone.

"About four hours."

Kim sighed. They drove in silence. Only the sound of the car's engine and tires kicking up small rocks on the road could be heard. The drive had been mostly quiet from the time they left the gas station to when they picked Aaliyah and Charlotte up from the pool hall. Rin took about five minutes to explain where they were going and why, and after that the inside of the car fell mute. There just didn't seem like much to say. Kim enjoyed the quiet, no questions, no lectures, no explanations that needed to be given, just quiet. But it could never last, nothing she enjoyed ever did.

"Hey?" Rin said staring out the passenger window.

"Hmmm?"

"What are we about to walk into right now?" she asked.

Her question took Kim off guard. She thought for a moment, but there was only one truthful answer.

"A trap more than likely," Kim answered.

Rin turned her head towards her.

"And we're just gonna walk right into it?"

Her tone was flat. She didn't sound upset, scared, or worried; the question passed over her lips no different than any normal question might.

"Do we have a choice Rin?" Kim asked in return.

She looked over and saw Rin palm her forehead as her lip began to quiver.

"Rin?" Kim whispered.

"I just," her voice began breaking, "I'm just thinking about Mom and Dad. If they saw us right now, what would they think, what would they say? If they knew the things we've done in our lives, done in this city…"

Kim took this as an indirect confession that Rin had failed to stay clean since moving to Joy City. She didn't blame her though, it wasn't her fault. No one stayed clean in Joy City.

"…in that alley…. I…. I don't know…"

"Stop, we both put that behind us years ago. And that, back there, that was self-defense, that's what you said Friday right? They were trying to kill us, we did what we had to."

Rin slumped down in her seat. Kim was a bit lost. Rin had seemed to be so emotionally composed up until the present moment.

"I just…. it's hard to believe this is our life right now," Rin murmured.

"For me, it's not really," Kim said pressing her lips together, "Before you showed up, this *was* my life. Not necessarily these exact same circumstances

194

but ridiculous stuff like this made up the years of my life I was in The Pool. To be honest with you, meeting me was probably the worst thing that could've ever happened to you."

"What?" Rin frowned, "that's not true, don't even..."

"No, really, this is what happens to people who associate themselves with me. Somehow, someway, they end up getting tangled up in this nightmare of a life I'm living. I told you about Joey, about LuLu and Cindy getting kidnapped, and here we are. I.... I just can't seem to keep people safe," her voice cracked as she spoke the last sentence.

"Kim, that's not your fault..."

"It is!" she snapped, slapping the steering wheel, "I promised myself when I started that mess that I wouldn't let anybody I loved be put in danger because of it.... but literally every single person close to me has."

She bit the inside of her jaw and took a long deep breath trying to compose herself. Even years after putting The Pool behind her, she still never fully forgave herself for the danger she put her loved ones in.

"I swear I'm like poison, anyone who even gets close to me ends up being affected somehow, someway. I'm sorry you..."

"Hey, no. I told you, I'm in this with you, no matter what."

"You.... you think..." Kim stuttered attempting to pull the words from her mouth, "....

Mom and Dad would be ashamed of us? You think they'd still love us if they knew…"

"No no no," Rin cut her off, "don't even start that. They were as loving as two people could be. They wouldn't have been proud of what we've done, but they would've still loved us no matter what, I know that for certain."

There was conviction in her words Kim wouldn't dare try to argue with.

"And, despite all, your foster parents would still love and be proud of you too," Rin added.

Her words sounded nice but Kim couldn't help but still feel ashamed.

"God, those people…. the life they gave me. I just wish I'd have gotten the chance to truly thank them for it."

"You lived pretty good separated from us for all those years huh?" Rin asked cracking a slight smile.

Kim wiped a few tears forming in the corner of her eye and sniffled.

"Tsk…. better than good. As a kid I grew accustomed to this lavish lifestyle I didn't even know I was living. Growing up in a foster home most of my life prior I assumed everyone with parents lived like I did. It wasn't really until I became a teenager and started hanging out at some of my friend's houses and around their families did I realize just how different I was actually living in comparison to them. We were living like royalty compared to the majority of Joy City."

"None of your friends ever teased you about being the pampered rich girl?"

"No one knew." Kim shrugged, "My foster parents made sure I knew right from wrong, took care of me but never spoiled me, and always made a big deal about treating everybody right regardless of what they had or didn't have. I wasn't raised to be stuck up or act like I was better than anyone else just cause we had some money. So, until my friends came to our house and saw the mansion and the cars and all that, none of them knew."

"That's good, they made sure not to let money corrupt you at an early age. Sounds like they were good people."

"They were *great* people. All the happiness I experienced during my childhood was the product of being adopted by them. For nearly ten years they gave me the most wonderful life a kid could ask for, a life I wouldn't have had a chance of living had they not."

"So, you were living like a princess, meanwhile we were waitin on Dad's food stamps to drop every month just so we could eat," Rin giggled.

Kim tried to fight a laugh that eventually broke through, "Oh yeah…. sorry," she said.

They both fell quiet. Rin looked into the backseat at Aaliyah and Charlotte sleeping. With the car silent again Kim began to think. So much had happened since she was first attacked in the parking lot of the grocery store. She was then brought back to the following day where Rin killed the man that tailed her from The Home. She remembered she hadn't so much as blinked as she committed the act.

After watching it happen, an unshakable thought entered Kim's head. When they first met Rin was far from comfortable with the act of killing, doing so only because she believed she had no other options. She now seemed capable of doing so without so much as batting an eye. While she couldn't prove it Kim believed her and Charlotte had trained more than just fitness over the years.

"Hey?" Kim asked.

Rin turned back around and faced her.

"Yeah?"

"You been handling yourself pretty well since all this mess started."

"What do you mean?" Rin asked.

"Defending yourself I mean. The guy that tailed me to your house, the attack at Aaliyah's place, the guy on the hill, those two earlier. When we fought four years ago you had some skill but not like that and you definitely didn't seem comfortable taking a life then."

Kim went quiet and discreetly shifted her eyes over to Rin whose face had turned.

Rin took a deep breath and exhaled heavily before she answered, "Ummm…. OK. So, here's the thing. You know Charlotte's been training me these past few years or whatever right?"

"Yeah."

"Well, that training kinda…. extended past fitness and exercise and all that…" Rin's timid voice told she wasn't ready to confess.

"Yeah? Extended to what?" Kim asked. She hid her slight grin on the other side of her face.

"Ummm.... well.... she said that if I was gonna stay in Joy City I should.... ummm..."

She stopped as she caught Kim biting her lip trying to keep from laughing.

"What?" Rin asked.

Kim shook her head as she giggled. Rin cut her eyes and twisted her lips into an annoyed smirk.

"...you already know," she said slowly.

"I've known Charlotte twice as long as you, I figured she was teaching you more than just exercise routines."

"You're not mad though?" Rin asked.

"I don't love it," she shrugged, "but realistically, had she not, you might not have survived this week."

Rin sucked her teeth and they shared a brief laugh.

"What about you? You been out of action for four years. If either of us wasn't gonna make it this week it was gonna be you."

"Out for four but I was in for six. You don't forget how to defend yourself once you know, especially when you end up teaching three others how to defend themselves too. Where do you think Charlotte learned everything she taught you?"

Rin cocked her head to the side having never really considered the thought previously.

"Knowing how to defend yourself in Joy City is not a bad thing, it's a necessity if anything really.

Just be careful, don't go lookin for fights, they're too easy to find back there," Kim told her.

Rin nodded as the screen on her phone lit up and played a cheerful tone that repeated three times. Rin smiled as she looked at the screen.

"What?" Kim asked.

"It's midnight," she said smiling at Kim.

Kim looked at her sideways unaware of what she found so significant about the time.

"OK…. and?"

Rin rolled her eyes at her.

"It's the eighteenth," Rin said, "Happy Birthday."

"Oh…. oh yeah, right, Happy Birthday," she said back to her.

Kim had always considered her birthday to be the tenth of January, the day she was first brought to The Home. With no birth certificate or records to tell her otherwise, as a child it was all she had. One day during the time she was still living with Kim, Rin revealed to her they were actually born on the eighteenth of May. After four years she still hadn't yet gotten used to her birthday occurring five months later than what she had believed it to be for over twenty years.

"Still weird huh?" Rin smiled.

"Yeah…"

"So much goin on I honestly forgot all about it."

"Yeah, me too."

Rin took a deep breath and let out a long huff of air.

"Well, we made thirty sis," she grinned.

"Yeah, yeah we did," she replied.

Kim was honestly a bit awestruck by it. You were considered lucky to make it to thirty in Joy City, and considered nearly immortal to make it to thirty in the line of work she was once in.

~

Kim stopped the car and placed it in park. She pressed the button to stop the engine and looked over at Rin.

"What's the time?"

"Four twenty-eight," she replied.

Kim turned around and looked at Aaliyah and Charlotte. They were both awake, staring curiously out the small window to Charlotte's left. Kim turned back around and looked out the window in the same direction. She saw one thing only; mountains. There was nothing else for miles. The coordinates had dropped them right in front of a humongous, zig zagging mountain range that seemed to go on forever in the direction they were heading. Where the range began to rise into the air was only a short distance from where they sat inside the car, and at the base of the range looked to be a small cave-like opening. Right in front of the opening sat a hooded figure in a long cloak.

"We lucked out tonight," Charlotte said, "the moon, the stars, without them we'd be out here in complete darkness."

"Darkness or not I wouldn't call where we're at right now lucky," Aaliyah said.

"Where are we anyway?" Rin asked.

"Gillidoux Rocks," Charlotte answered, "a giant mountain range that stretches from here all the way through to the next state. When the coordinates started taking us into the desert, I thought we might end up here, but why is the question."

"Whoever that is," Kim said opening the door, "I'm sure they know."

Kim got out of the car and pulled the seat up to let Charlotte out. Rin and Aaliyah exited from the other side. The air was cold, the soundtrack that accompanied it was mute aside from a few stray whips of wind. They were truly in the middle of nowhere.

Before slamming the door shut, Kim grabbed the sickle she picked up in the alley from underneath the seat. She tucked it into the back of her pants and glared at the figure still sitting motionless in front of the hole in the mountainside. Rin, Aaliyah, and Charlotte all fixed their eyes on the figure and huddled around her.

"Hey," Rin began, "what if they're just the bait to spring the trap?"

Without a word Kim began marching forward directly towards where the hooded figure sat.

"Wh-Kim?" Rin gasped.

She ignored her and continued walking. Rin looked over to Charlotte.

"When chica's on a mission, she's hard to get through to," she shrugged.

202

"There could be a whole army waitin to ambush us in that cave."

"She knows, I don't think she cares though," Aaliyah said following after her.

Charlotte shrugged again and followed behind Aaliyah. Rin fell in line as well. Once she was about twenty or so yards away from the mouth of the cave Kim stopped, allowing the others to catch up. The figure remained still almost as if unaware of their arrival. Kim looked up and noticed a ledge that appeared to wrap up and around the side of the range. It looked wide enough to travel, almost like a path. It seemed out of place with the rest of the range's jagged makeup.

"Think that's him, the voice on the recordings?" Charlotte asked.

"Doubt it, he's not runnin his mouth enough for that to be him," Aaliyah said.

"Hey!?" Kim called out.

Finally acknowledging their presence, the figure raised its hooded head and stood. The person was tall, Kim assumed it was another man. He was drowning in the black cloak wrapped around his body. Kim noticed his right sleeve was much longer than the left and flared out in an odd fashion at its end. Motionless, he stood across from them as if waiting for something. Kim found the sight of him a bit chilling, almost as if standing across from the grim reaper himself.

"Are you…"

Before Kim could finish her sentence, he fell into a sprint directly towards them. Kim gasped and braced to defend herself.

"This again huh?" Charlotte grunted bracing herself as well.

"Stay back, we don't know what he's capable of," Kim called over her shoulder.

She tucked her chain in and pulled the sickle from her backside. She hurled it towards him as he charged at her. It spun wildly in the air as it flew. Just as it was about to make contact, he effortlessly brushed it away with a swipe of his arm. The sickle went careening to the left. He never broke stride, quickly closing the space between them. Kim pulled her hair pick from her side and rushed forward.

"Kim no!" she heard Rin's voice behind her.

Once in range she threw a punch with the pick's blade poking out between her fingers but it whiffed high. He went low and slid into her feet knocking her to her knees. She quickly rose and threw an elbow hard behind her. He did the same and the back of their arms met in a clash. As they struggled against each other Kim was able to catch a glimpse of the man's face underneath his hood. It was extremely boney with a thin long goatee hanging down from under his bottom lip. The expression on his face was chilling; absent of any emotion.

A light roar suddenly came from behind him. He quickly shoved Kim hard sending her flying onto her back. He turned around, and with his right arm blocked a downward strike from the sword Rin had picked up from the night before. Rin froze when the blade made contact with his arm and emitted a loud clanking sound. He wiped the blade away, knocking it out of her hand. He delivered a quick jab to Rin's gut with his left hand. She hunched over grabbing her stomach as he dropped a heavy elbow onto her back. She stumbled back, eventually crumbling to the ground.

Aaliyah and Charlotte then both attacked him in unison. They came from opposite sides throwing several punches and low kicks but each either missed or was blocked. Just as he did to Rin, he quickly jabbed Charlotte in her stomach, grabbed her arm, and pulled her across his body. Charlotte grabbed hold of his flared sleeve as he tossed her into Aaliyah's arms. Aaliyah caught her but spun wildly in place attempting to stay on her feet. Charlotte kept her hold of the man's sleeve and as they spun it tore at the flared end and exposed his right hand. On it he wore a metal gauntlet that went more than halfway up his forearm. It looked like something out of a horror film. Positioned over each of his fingers was a small vial filled with a green substance and on the end of each vial were long sharp needles. A thin clear tube ran from each vial to the metal base of the gauntlet with the same green fluid running through them.

Aaliyah and Charlotte stared at the gauntlet with a mix of awe and confusion. The man then raised his arm over his head and quickly slashed down at them. Aaliyah instinctively turned her body away shielding Charlotte from the attack. The gauntlet's needles scored her left shoulder. She immediately screamed and threw Charlotte down. She grabbed at her arm and fell to her knees.

Charlotte quickly crawled over to her and pried her hand from where the needles had scraped her. They had sliced right through her clothes, leaving cuts on her arm. Charlotte's mouth fell open as she examined them. The cuts were thin but deep, each one dripping a brown fluid; the green substance of the vials mixing with her blood. Aaliyah's breaths began to grow short and heavy as she began to shake and twitch uncontrollably. Charlotte's eyes lit up, she cursed aloud, and whipped her head around towards Kim and Rin.

"There's poison in those needles, don't let them touch you!" she yelled.

"Poison?" Kim whispered to herself.

Before she could finish the thought the man turned around and extended his arm clawing at her. She rolled backwards and onto her feet barely avoiding the swipe. She tried to punish his miss by kicking him low but he caught her leg holding it up against his. She threw a quick right hook but he ducked under it. As he rose back up he chopped down hard on Kim's leg at the knee. Her leg hyperextended and she shrieked before yanking her leg free from his grasp. She hopped backwards on one leg, eventually collapsing to the ground. Rin then rushed him again from behind.

"Rin, get back!" Charlotte called out to her.

Rin ignored her and continued her sprint towards him. She threw a tireless series of jabs and punches, none landed. Her final swing went so far over the man's head he grabbed her arm and slung her outwards. She twirled away from him struggling to keep her balance. As she recovered, she threw an off balanced back fisted punch behind herself and spun around to face him but he wasn't there. She spun around again trying to locate him and took an uppercut right under her chin. Flying backwards, she landed hard on her back.

The man looked around ensuring no one else was still daring enough to challenge him. They couldn't touch him and they knew it. Hand to hand he was in a league of his own, even more so than the others they had encountered. He turned back towards Rin and walked her down until he stood right over her. Kim pushed herself up onto one knee. Her leg was still throbbing. The man raised his hand, strumming the air with his fingers, letting the tips of the needle's tips click against each other. Kim looked over and made eye contact with Charlotte. She shook her head begging her to stay down.

Kim pushed off from her crouched position, ran, and dove at the man with her pick's blade extended out. It was an act of pure desperation. In the blink of an eye the man turned around, sidestepped, and quickly slashed at her. She caught his gauntlet's needles across her stomach. She landed on a knee in front of him and whined aloud feeling a sharp sting where the needles touched her. She tucked her pick back at her side and collapsed from her knee on to all fours. He took a step towards her as she threw her arm out hard behind her. She made contact with his arm causing the gauntlet to slip off his hand. It went flying through the air before landing in the dirt a few yards away from them.

Kim lifted her jacket up just enough to see her stomach. She saw four deep gashes across her abdominal area. Each one dripping a brown mixture of blood and poison. Kim's heart started racing as her body began heating up, breathing became difficult, and she began involuntarily twitching. She grew slightly dizzy and a pain began swelling in her head.

"Kim, get up!" Rin desperately urged her.

Before she could find the strength to do anything, Kim was yanked up by her collar. The man picked her up and held her suspended in the air. She tried to get another look at his face under the hood but still wasn't able to see much. What little she could see was a cold, desolate expression. She raised her arm and grabbed his wrist but there was no strength in her grip. Her arm was trembling, her entire body felt weak. The poison was spreading at an alarming rate. Within just a few seconds it had rendered her mostly fatigued.

The man slowly raised his free hand for what she believed to be a killing blow. She tried to shake herself free but couldn't muster the strength; she was gassed. She bit down on her bottom lip and shut her eyes, bracing for impact but a sound came first, a thud. Kim immediately opened her eyes and saw a small rock had bounced off the man's shoulder and fallen to the ground behind him. He spun his head around looking up towards one of the lower peaks of the mountain range's rise. His focus went to a hanging cliff that had to be at least two hundred or so feet above them. On the edge stood a similarly cloaked figure. All eyes fixated on it.

Suddenly the man released his grip, dropping Kim hard on the ground. Rin immediately scrambled over to her.

The man turned his back on them and growled, "He'll see you now."

There was anger in his voice. It sounded as though he had spoken through clinched teeth. But his voice was light, no lisp, he wasn't the one on the recordings. Slowly he began to walk away. He left an ominous aura in the air. They all watched in awe as he withdrew from them. As he got further into the distance all their eyes met at once sharing the same pitiful gaze.

"Wh-what the hell?" Aaliyah panted.

Kim pushed Rin off of her as she struggled onto her feet.

"Hey careful," Rin warned her.

Kim's knees buckled, she couldn't seem to find air to breathe, her entire body felt tense and sore.

"Yo, look at this," Charlotte said crouched over the man's gauntlet, "this is insane."

Aaliyah, with a tight grip on her shoulder, stood and took slow steps over toward where she was. Rin helped Kim gingerly inch over as well.

"What is that?" Rin asked.

"It looks like a mechanized gauntlet with vials pumping highly concentrated poison into the tips of needles," Charlotte answered.

"What?!" Aaliyah panted with a look of horror on her face.

"I.... I don't even know. This isn't normal weaponry, this is stuff you see in comic books," she said shaking her head.

Kim again shoved Rin away and stood up straight. She let out a small cry and quickly placed her hands over where she had been cut.

"Hey take it easy!" Rin said.

She turned to Charlotte.

"What can you do about this poison, it seems like it's workin fast."

".... nothin really," she said shaking her head.

"What?! What do you mean nothin?!" Rin cried.

"We're in the middle of the desert Rin! All we got is gauze, alcohol, and bandages. You can't treat poison with that!"

Rin sucked her teeth and cursed aloud.

"From the looks of it, this stuff is way more potent than anything I know how to treat anyway. Even if we were back home I don't know how much I'd be able to do."

There was fear in Charlotte's voice, they all heard it. It was unnerving. They all knew her and knew she wasn't one to succumb to fear.

"So then what, they just gotta deal with it, hope we make it back to the city before it kills them?!" Rin cried.

"What else can we do Rin?!" she barked back.

"We're not going back," Kim huffed.

"What?" Rin cried.

Kim bent over where the gauntlet rested on the ground and snatched one of the poison vials from its socket. She tucked it at her side next to her hair pick.

"We're going to the top of that cliff…. I am anyway."

She began limping forward towards the cave.

"What? Kim?" Rin called to her. She caught up to her, grabbed her shoulder, and spun her around. Kim snatched herself from her grip but immediately hunched over in pain.

"Exactly, there's no way we're goin up there with you two like this, you can't defend yourselves anymore…"

"So what then?! You wanna go back to Joy City to be hunted down like animals?!"

Her voice was harsh, slicing through the silent air around them. Rin shrunk a bit, as she always did when Kim reminded her who was the eldest.

"This is gonna end right now, somehow, someway, with whoever or whatever is at the top of that cliff. I'm not living another day of my life like this. If you want to you can stay here but you said you were in this with me, right?"

Rin's silence served as her guilty answer. Kim turned away from her and continued to march forward grunting with each painful step. As she hobbled along, she looked up at the figure on the cliff with fire in her eyes. She was done running, done hiding, and done allowing her past to control her present and future. She wanted her freedom and she believed it was to be claimed at the top of the cliff.

Poisoned or not, turning back wasn't an option for her. She was ready to be done, ready to be free.

"Uhhh…"

Kim looked to her right and saw Helena walking step for step with her.

"… K, you might wanna listen to little sis just this once. That's a pretty high climb and you're barely standing right now. Turning back might be…"

"Leave me alone," Kim angrily panted.

Helena sighed.

"You know I can't." There was a rare desperation in her voice, "K, you're in bad shape right now, please just…"

Kim stopped and shot her a glare so ugly Helena hushed herself. She conceded and dropped her head. Kim turned from her and continued walking.

Helena closed her eyes, sighed, and crossed her arms, "Alright, birthday girl, have it your way."

Chapter 8

Kim IIII

Rin tucked the sword she was carrying under her arm and pulled out her burner phone.

"5:53" she read the time silently.

Rin, Aaliyah, and Charlotte all stood behind Kim as she looked out the mouth of the cave they stood in. They had entered the cave from the bottom and ascended up the spiraling path that wrapped around the mountainside. It was narrow and steep but they followed it, eventually coming to another cavern-like opening in the mountainside. They entered and walked through until they saw light again where the cave opened back up. The opening led out to a cliff, and standing at the edge of the cliff, what they hoped to be the end to the madness.

Aaliyah trembled in Charlotte's arms as they stood. The poison had rendered her nearly helpless. She was sweating bullets, gasping for air, and had to be shaken a few times on the way up the path to keep from passing out.

"Hey hey, look at me," Charlotte said shaking her arm, "you OK?"

Aaliyah nodded yes, but her yellowing eyes and disoriented gaze told her a liar. Charlotte looked to Rin at her right and noticed the worry in her expression.

"Ugh…. mierda." Charlotte groaned under her breath, "I don't know how Kim's still standing right now, she took more than her and she can barely keep her feet under her."

Rin turned her attention to Kim standing hobbled in front of them.

"Somehow her will to survive is beatin that poison, for now anyway," she said.

Kim's body was at war with her mind. Physically she was drained, but mentally, emotionally, she couldn't yield. She looked back over her shoulder and locked eyes with each of them. Their silence was all the affirmation she needed to continue. With a limp in her step she walked forward out of the cave's shade and into the dawn light.

The cliff sloped downward a bit from the mouth of the cave. Kim had to watch every step she made, carefully stepping over and around the rocky terrain beneath her feet. Each step took an immense amount of energy and concentration. She was fatigued beyond belief, her head was pounding, she was seeing double, sweating profusely, and the altitude's thin air made breathing a more than difficult task. The sting from the gashes across her stomach had grown more intense as well. They were burning as if something had set fire to them. Still, she kept herself upright, she kept moving forward. All she could see was what stood between her and her freedom, a cloaked figure standing on the edge of a cliff.

"Kim, stop, please," Helena whined stepping in front of her.

Kim frowned in her face.

"Just listen alright?" Helena glanced over her shoulder at the man, "I really don't think you should be steppin to this guy."

Kim's nostrils flared and she let out a low growl.

"I'm just sayin, this guy's waitin on a mountaintop, you couldn't even beat the guy at the steps. And now..."

She lifted up Kim's jacket revealing the lacerations across her stomach. They looked much worse than they had before. Each had begun to discharge a thick yellow pus and the skin around them looked to be shriveling up and drying out.

"... you're banged up, you're poisoned, is this really how you wanna spend your birthday?"

Kim knocked her hand down and looked her off as she tried to move around her. Again, Helena quickly stepped in her path. Her eyes were big, but not with their usual excitement or joy.

"Kim, please…. I've never asked you for anything before but I'm asking you now, please don't…"

Kim brushed her aside and continued forward. Helena watched as the others followed behind her like soldiers.

Kim stopped when she was just a few feet from the cloaked figure. Rin, Aaliyah, and Charlotte stopped just behind her. The figure stood with their back to them. The tail and sleeves of the cloak along with a long scarf whipped wildly in the breeze. The figures hood then slowly turned to the side.

"Hmph…." he chuckled to himself, "been waitin a long time for you."

Each word was spoken slowly, through a lisp, behind a southern accent. It was him, the voice on the recordings. Kim's skin began to crawl, his voice was even more unpleasant to the ear in person. His hood turned back, facing the cliff's edge.

"You ladies look a little beat up. Hope my buddy didn't give y'all too much trouble down there. I told him to be careful, keep y'all alive but…. looked like he might've forgot for a second."

Again, his hood turned and he extended his arm out to the side. In his hand he held half a cigarette.

"Smoke?" he asked over his shoulder.

None of them answered. He shrugged, pulled his arm back, and turned his head forward again.

"You girls came all this way just to see me, I'm touched."

"Enough." Charlotte stepped forward. "Who are you, why are we here, and what do you want?"

The man took a deep breath exhaling from his mouth. He flicked his cigarette over the cliff and into the wind.

"Yeah…. I guess I owe y'all that," he said.

Slowly he spun around to face them. The cloak he wore was draped over his front as well stretching all the way down to the ground. All black everything; he looked like a shadow standing upright, except for his face. It was still halfway covered inside the shadow of his hood, but what they could see of it was chilling. His face was long and thin. His chin was protruded forward, sticking out from the rest of his face. His nose was pointy and rigid. His skin was beyond pale, it almost looked gray, full of blotches and dark spots. The one of his eyes that was exposed was yellow and bloodshot. Topping off his dreadful appearance was a wide, crooked smile stretching from ear to ear.

"Crain, that's what they call me."

He looked back and forth between the four of them waiting for a response. He chuckled at their silence

"So why then right? Why are you here? Should be obvious. What's the reason for everything that's happened to y'all in the past decade?"

They all knew the answer.

"Hmph.... talkative little things aren't y'all." he smirked, "So then what? What's the reason for the why?"

His hands suddenly emerged from inside his cloak. He held a lighter in one and another cigarette in the other. He lit the cigarette and placed it in between his dry cracked lips. He inhaled, paused, and smoke barreled out from his nostrils. He took the cigarette from his mouth, holding it between his fingers. His devious smile faded in an instant.

"Kim, your parent's, the one's that adopted you, their deaths are the reason we're all standing on this rock right now."

Kim's eyes grew wide.

"Twenty-five years ago, give or take a few, the worst thing that ever happened to Joy City happened, born by the hands of your parents and one of their oldest friends. Why?" he shrugged, "I don't know, the excuse I always heard, they just needed money. The need for money will cause a person to do things they'd never have imagined themselves capable of, make them step out of their character entirely."

His voice went soft; he seemed to strike a nerve within himself.

"My father fell victim to this unfortunate fate. I was just a little boy when he joined them." he gently shook his head, "He didn't know it then but.... it was the worst decision he'd ever make in his life."

He took another puff from his cigarette and continued.

"Things actually ran smooth for the better part of a decade, but your father was a bit too careless and got himself and your mother killed." he shook his head again in disgust, "A shame really. I liked them, they were good people, you were lucky to have them for the time you did."

His tone was genuine as he spoke praise of her foster parents. They were obviously somewhat acquainted, she wondered what they thought of him.

"A month or so after they were killed The Pool fell. Our fathers were close Kim. You probably don't remember but we played together a few times as kids.

My father brought me to a couple of your birthday parties when we were younger."

The thought sent chills up her spine.

"They never figured out exactly who was responsible for your parents' murder but somehow they deduced it had something to do with The Pool. My father, loving yours like a brother, couldn't stomach it. Everyone in that pool hall was like family to him. He motioned for The Pool to cease operation right then, out of respect for the brother and sister they'd lost because of it. All were in favor, the man who tailed you from the foster home Saturday, the four who attacked you in the house, the woman you.... killed at the store Tuesday..."

His voice trembled as he spoke her fate.

"... the man you fought on the hill, the two you dueled last night, and the one you met on the ground; The Pool about fifteen years ago."

Kim was surprised hearing The Pool had so many members previously.

"Everyone agreed the only way to truly honor your parents' death was for The Pool to die along with them, everyone except Terrance."

He had all their eyes and ears. None of them dared interrupt.

"Whether he was driven by the money or just fell in love with havin other people's blood on his hands, he opposed my father's suggestion and lashed out at him for even makin it. They went back and forth, arguing and such until Terrance had enough and dismissed him. Told him he was no longer welcome inside the pool hall. My father's response as he left.... a threat, a threat to expose The Pool and all its doings. Terrance had him killed before the sun rose the next day."

Kim was stunned. She knew little to nothing of The Pool's years or its members prior to her joining. Though she always noticed the comfort Terrance found in their small group. While she paid it no mind then she was now beginning to wonder had there been an intentionality behind their small numbers.

"That was the final straw, that caused the fall. After seeing how quick he was to have someone he called his brother murdered for simply disagreeing with him, all the others walked, and The Pool seemed destined to soon be all but a bad memory for those involved. They figured he couldn't run it alone, not for long anyway. They all assumed he'd either work himself to death tryin, or get himself killed in the process, so they all just moved on."

He raised his cigarette back up to his lips and took a long huff before again blowing smoke out his nose.

"About ten years later, Christmas Day, I took a visit to see my Aunt Rose, the woman you.... met at the grocery store. She took me in after my father's murder, she was the closest thing I've had to family since. I walked inside her house and found her crying in front of the TV. The news was on, and the headline read 'abandoned pool hall in woods found occupied'."

His horrid smile returned alongside a small chuckle.

"See, initially I was kept in the dark about my father's murder, I was told he was the victim of a random act of violence, you know…. Joy City?" he shrugged, "But that day, she told me everything. Y'all don't know how bad it hurt to find out the man I once thought of as family was the one responsible for my father's murder. That was a sad Christmas for us. I cried, Aunt Rose cried, we cried, until neither of us had any more tears left. Then we looked at each other and she saw in my eyes the same thing I saw in hers, a broken heart that needed mending. She made a call, then she made another, and then she made a few more. In a week or so we had a house full of people disgusted with the way things ended in that pool hall. In a month or two we had a common mind that as late as it was, something needed to be done about it. A few years later we had a plan to make Terrance regret everything he'd done to us…"

"So all this is because of a grudge you have against Terrance, this ain't even about us, is it?" Charlotte asked.

Crain again chuckled under his breath.

"I'm sorry…. did you actually think somethin different? Y'all didn't really think this was about *you,* did you? C'mon, you think had The Pool outlived you all and some other poor misguided souls replaced you I wouldn't still be here staring someone down? You're all just a part of a game much bigger than yourselves. Your names may be on the box, but inside, you're nothin but a novelty. In ten years, in five, who would've remembered your names inside that pool hall? See, the game's the thing, The Pool, what writes the never ending story. Had you died before it, that story would've just began all over again."

"So then why go after us and not him?" Charlotte asked.

"We all suffered fifteen years ago…. losin someone we loved," he flicked his cigarette forward.

Kim watched as it spun in the air and eventually hit the ground just inches from her foot.

"It's time he suffered too."

Crain quickly lunged forward and punched Kim in her gut. The blow knocked the wind out of her. She heard a collective of gasps from behind as she collapsed to her knees struggling to breathe. She looked up just as Crain's foot made contact with her face. As she tipped over she heard shuffling on the ground from all directions around her. The side of her face hit the ground hard and she blacked out to the sound of Rin and Charlotte struggling.

~

Kim slowly opened her eyes. She felt groggy, lying on her side. She lifted her face up from the ground and looked around. She immediately noticed she was no longer atop the cliff. She was still on desert ground but a now completely flat area that seemed to go on forever in all directions. She looked up and noticed storm clouds had taken over the sky. She hadn't remembered seeing any before. She wondered how long she had been out.

She propped herself up on her elbow and scanned the desert plains. To her surprise she looked to be alone; no sign of Crain, Rin, Aaliyah, or Charlotte. Listening she heard nothing. It was eerily quiet, even for a desert. She lifted up her shirt and ran her fingers over her stomach. There were no scars. She felt no pain in her leg either. She was beyond confused.

"Rin?!" she called out.

There was no answer. She pressed herself up onto her knees and looked all around. The desert looked more barren than she recalled. All she could see was dry cracked terrain for miles.

"Kim..." a deep voice behind her breathed.

She turned around and her heart skipped a beat. Standing in front of her were her foster parents, dressed in the clothes they were buried in fifteen years ago. They looked down at her with shameful stares.

"Mom.... Dad?" she whimpered with tears in her eyes.

"Why Kim?" her foster father spoke in a harsh tone, "Why did you let The Pool fall?"

Kim was thrown by his question. Her mouth hung open.

"What? I.... I didn't..."

"We worked so hard to build The Pool, for you, how could you let it die?" her foster mother chimed in.

"N-no.... it wasn't my fault.... I..."

"Everything we did for you and this is how you repay us, by allowing the legacy we left to you to rot?

You were supposed to continue what we couldn't, you failed us Kim," her foster father continued.

"Everything we did, we did because we loved you, did you not love us back?" her foster mother asked.

Their questions weighed heavy on her. She couldn't handle seeing the disappointment in their eyes as they stared down at her. She began to second guess all the things she believed she had come to terms with years ago. Was The Pool's fall ultimately her fault? Had she only been adopted to be bred into it? Had the plan always been for her to eventually be a part of it?

"I-I'm…." tears began rolling down her cheeks, ".... I'm sorry, I…"

"Kim…" another shaky voice came from behind her.

She turned around and saw her biological parents. They were both just as she remembered them Christmas morning four years ago.

"Mom…. Dad?" she whimpered again.

"Kim…" her mother began.

There were tears in her eyes, her voice was trembling, and on her face was a horrified worrisome stare. Her father shared the same look.

".... an assassin?" her mother cried.

Kim again fell mute to shame.

"Kim, how could you? How could you kill people for money?" she cried.

Kim's lip began to quiver. She was at a loss for words.

"Kim," her father spoke in a pitiful voice, "how can you live with yourself having done this? How?"

"I don't…. I…" she stuttered.

"I'm so disappointed in you," her mother cried as she covered her face.

Kim's spirit was crushed. She hadn't known her biological parents for more than an hour, but if there had been anything she wanted from them, it was for them to be proud of her. Mentally, emotionally, she couldn't handle them being disappointed in her.

"No…. no, Mom, please…" she cried reaching out toward them.

They both cowered back stepping out of her reach as though afraid of her. The sight caused her to begin crying even harder.

"No, please," she panted.

"Kim," her foster father spoke from behind her, "the Pool was our legacy, your destiny, and you let it go."

"You threw away everything we built for you," her foster mother added.

"You're not my daughter, you're a monster," her biological mother huffed.

"I can't believe you ended up like this," her biological father sighed.

Kim curled herself into a ball, hugged her knees, and began rocking back and forth anxiously. She sat in the middle of her four parents as they scolded her, each word they uttered cutting her deeper and deeper. She started bawling, torn between

225

right and wrong, two sets of differing opinions, and love, so much love.

Talking over one another, both sets of her parents relentlessly condemned her. She could feel herself breaking down. Her head began pounding, her vision went fuzzy, she broke into a sweat, and all her muscles tensed up. She began to shake uncontrollably and the harsh stinging pain over her stomach returned. Everything around her went dark and the voices stopped.

In an instant her eyes opened and her head jerked up from the ground. She was panting, gasping for air. She felt like she had just run a mile. She looked up at the sky and noticed the same storm clouds above. Looking around, she was still in the desert but now in what appeared to be some sort of shallow valley. From where she laid, she could look up and see the mountaintop and cliff. She wondered how she had gotten down. She knew she couldn't have walked herself.

She tried to press herself up but fell back flat, she had no strength. She reached down and gently ran her fingers over her stomach feeling the four gashes across it. The pain was excruciating.

She eventually was able to force herself onto her hands and knees. A few yards away from her she saw Rin on her back holding her side. A bit to her left she saw Charlotte on her stomach struggling to rise. Just to her right she saw Aaliyah's body lying motionless; she was completely still. Kim feared the worst for her. She struggled as she slowly rose up. As

226

she got to her feet she stood hunched over with her arms hanging as she fought her body's exhaustion.

Rin lifted her head and a look of awe came over her face. Kim noticed she wasn't looking at her though, but something behind her. Kim turned around and towering over her stood Crain. He had removed the cloak he had been wearing before. He was shirtless wearing only a pair of baggy black pants. Now uncloaked, she was able to get a good look at his truly horrifying appearance.

He was as thin as a skeleton. She could practically see every bone in his body underneath his skin. His head was bald and resting above his yellow eyes were two paper-thin eyebrows. His skin was truly as gray as it had looked atop the cliff under his hood. From his face down to his torso, his skin looked disease-ridden, riddled with discolored blotches, bumps, and scars. He looked horribly sick. At first glance he could be mistaken for someone who was already dead.

She hadn't realized before just how much taller than her he was. Though much skinnier he was a giant compared to her. He stared down at her with a repulsive glare. She returned it with a nasty gaze of her own. He then delivered a crushing kick to her side that sent her flying until she crashed hard into the valley wall.

"Kim!" she heard Rin scream in the distance.

The kick's impact felt like it paralyzed her entire body. She couldn't so much as lift her head from the ground. Crain slowly walked over and pulled her up by her hair. He stood her up and punched her hard in her face. Her head snapped back into the wall behind her. She hunched over and saw several drops of blood drip from her nose onto the ground. She heard a small chuckle from Crain and then felt the weight of his elbow slamming down onto her back. She collapsed flat onto the ground. He then picked her up by one arm and one leg and tossed her into the air. She landed hard and rolled back onto her stomach.

Her body felt numb, any part of it that she could still feel was in an immense amount of pain. It hurt to even breathe. With a trembling hand she ran one of her fingers under her nose and felt the blood running from her nostrils. She held the finger out in front of her face and shivered. Although she could already smell and taste it, something about seeing the blood on her fingertips shook her.

"Kim, hold on!" she heard Rin's voice cry among the rattling in her ear.

Kim's eyes drifted to her right and she saw the short sword Rin had brought up the mountain resting on the ground. Slowly she began reaching her arm out towards its handle. The further her arm reached the more pain she felt. She placed a single finger on the handle just as Crain's foot stomped down on her wrist. A horrible pain shot up her arm, to her back, and all the way down her spine. She let out a miserable cry. He lifted his foot from off her wrist, grabbed her up by her neck, and held her suspended in the air. She looked down at him and on his face was the most villainous smile she had ever seen in her life. He was finding joy in torturing her.

"Hmph...." he grinned up at her, "don't worry, I'll let Terrance know you girls gave it your best shot."

His smile quickly faded as he heard footsteps coming from behind him. Rin, with a limp, charged at him. She scooped the short sword up from the ground but before she could swing it he extended his leg out and his foot caught her in her stomach. She dropped the sword and collapsed to a knee. Crain dropped Kim flat onto her back. He then roundhouse kicked Rin in the face sending her sliding backwards. He bent over, picked up the sword, and began walking her down.

Kim stared up at the sky motionless. For a moment she believed she was already dead. Every bone in her body ached, every muscle felt sore, her breaths appeared to be slowing by the second, and she could barely see anything through her blurred vision. She felt physically and emotionally wrecked. She kept running the story Crain told atop the cliff over and over again in her head, she couldn't believe it. She couldn't believe Terrance, she couldn't believe herself, she couldn't believe her life. Everything she had been through, to end up lying on her back helpless in the desert, a victim of a revenge tour.

She then thought about Cindy, LuLu, Blake, Ms. C, Rin, and couldn't imagine never seeing them again, she couldn't imagine these being her final moments. Though she didn't believe she deserved much, she did believe she deserved better than this.

Against everything her body and mind told her, she took a deep breath and slowly sat up. Through her blurred vision, she saw Crain walking Rin down as she laid defenseless on the ground. Kim suddenly recalled the promise she made to their parents the day they were laid to rest.

I promise I'll take care of Rin, we'll be OK.

She reached at her side and pulled her hair pick and the vial of poison she tucked next to it. She slammed the bottom of the vial down on the ground next to her and it shattered. The poison began oozing out the vial forming a small green puddle on the ground. She carefully rolled her pick's blade in it ensuring it was fully coated.

Crain, now standing over Rin, smiled as he looked down on her. She rolled over and scooted herself away from him.

"It's unfortunate you had to be here for this, truth is you didn't have to be. You weren't a part of the problem, but you just couldn't keep your nose out of other people's business could you?" he said pointing the sword at her.

"Anything involving my sister is my business," Rin grunted back at him.

"Fair enough," he shrugged, "if you wanna go down with her over this be my guest, one more of you isn't..."

The sound of shuffling across the dry land immediately hushed Crain. He whipped his head around and saw Kim standing just a few feet from him. Before he could react she threw her hand out and a dust cloud of dirt and small rocks flew toward him. Crain raised his forearm shielding his face. With the last bit of strength she had left Kim jabbed for his gut with her pick's blade extended between her fingers. Crain caught her wrist and twisted it as he pulled her arm up over her head. He spun her around and stuck the sword into her back and through her stomach.

"Kim!" Rin screamed.

Her voice echoed throughout the valley so loud Charlotte raised her head. Her eyes grew twice in size and her mouth fell open as she stared in shock. Kim lost her breath as she stared down at the sword's tip. She dropped her pick and gently wrapped her hands around the blade as she nervously shook.

"Sorry," Crain whispered with a smile, "left yourself wide open."

He put his foot on her back and kicked her forward as he pulled the sword out of her. The sword zipped through her hands leaving deep lacerations in her palms. Her body ragdolled as it dropped to the ground. Charlotte shivered before finally looking away. Crain proudly smiled as he stood over her.

"You monster!" Rin wailed.

She quickly sprang to her feet and rushed him swinging a wild right hook. He sidestepped, tripped, and flipped her over onto her back. She rolled over writhing in pain. Kim, still conscious, heard her cries and a single tear began rolling down her cheek.

"Hmph…. well, you both look tapped." he looked over to where Charlotte was lying and smiled, "How about you Charlotte, you still alive over there?!"

His voice loud and pompous as he taunted them. He turned his back to Kim and Rin and began to stroll over towards her. Rin, laying on her stomach, tried to press herself up. As she placed her right hand on the ground she felt something under it; something light, and still warm.

Kim could only watch in horror. She didn't have the strength to move a single muscle. The poison had worked its way through her and rendered her entire body weak. She was now rapidly losing blood. She knew it; she was done. As she watched Crain walk Charlotte down helplessness set in. They had come so far, overcome so much, just to lose. Pain was subduing from her body; she was starting to lose all feeling completely. She couldn't remember a time ever feeling so hopeless in her life, she was broken in every aspect of her being.

This is it, she thought to herself, *this is where it ends.*

A blur of red and black suddenly came into her peripheral. A pair of red sneakers and black socks she had become familiar with. Kim looked up and saw what might as well have been a complete stranger; Helena, with her eyes full of tears and a pitiful pout on her face. She dropped down to her knees next to Kim and placed a hand on her back. She was shaking anxiously as she looked over Kim's body.

The sight was wildly unfamiliar, Helena had never looked so emotionally struck. Her eyes told Kim she was beyond worried, she was terrified. The slightest of smiles came across Kim's face. The look startled Helena causing her to draw back a bit.

"I-I guess this makes one huh?" Kim whispered grinning.

Her voice was so soft, she didn't have the strength or breath to put anything but air behind her words.

"What?" Helena asked.

Kim's grin grew a bit wider and she let out a small giggle that ended in a sickly cough.

"Monday.... you said whatever happens, I'd make it out on the other side. Well.... looks like you were finally wrong about something.... I don't think I'm makin it outta this one."

Helena's pout turned into an open-mouthed stare.

"Kim no.... don't.... don't say that..." she cried, wiping her tears.

Kim stared deep into her eyes.

"I love you Helena.... thank you again.... for everything."

"Kim..." Helena gently shook her, "stop, d-don't do that..."

"Hey.... can I ask my offset for one last favor?"

Helena leaned in close to her.

"You told me.... if your fate was ever in your own hands, and you couldn't help me, you'd just wanna help the next person who needed you, right? Helena, please.... help Rin.... she's gonna need you."

"What?" Helena responded looking over to Rin.

Rin struggled pushing herself up from the ground. She first made it to a knee, then stood, and began slowly limping after Crain.

"Hey!" she called out to him.

He froze and looked back over his shoulder.

"Me and you aren't done yet!" she groaned.

Crain sighed and shook his head as he spun around to face her.

"Can't you see I'm tryin to let you live girl? This ain't about you, just get outta here."

She continued closing the space between them until she was but an arm's length away from him.

"The moment you hurt my sister this became about me..."

In the blink of an eye Crain reached out and grabbed Rin's neck. He lifted her into the air and began choking her. Rin grabbed his wrist but couldn't make him release his grip.

"Look, I get it. I'm sorry your sister and her friends made the decisions they made, but truthfully if anyone's to blame here it's Terrance. His actions are the reason we're here, the reason your sister is poisoned with a hole in her stomach right now. It's unfortunate that so many are going to have to suffer for the sins of just one but don't worry, I promise, as soon as we wrap this up here, he's next, and I'll make sure that he suffers the most for what he's cost us all, but that suffering had to start somewhere, and this is where, the loss of all his little replacement assassins."

He smiled up at her as she continued fighting against his grip. They stared between each other for a moment until Crain's smile faded away. He closed his eyes, bowed his head, and sighed.

"I wanna let you go, you're innocent in this matter, but you seem to have a death wish. You have my word though, I'll make Terrance suffer for all of this. For my father, for your sister even, everyone, everyone he got tangled up in that damn pool hall."

On his face now, a hard frown. He looked angry. He bowed his head, tightly shut his eyes, pressed his lips together, and scrunched up his nose.

"We're cursed you and I, to have ties to Joy City, ties to The Pool, to be here right now. It could've been any two people in the world in this very spot we are right now, but it's us. We have to be cursed. I can assure you I hate this just as much as you do, but that's why it has to happen."

He tightened his grip on her neck. She couldn't breathe, she began to squirm.

"So now ends this chapter of the story, and on to the next..."

He abruptly fell silent following a small grunt. He opened his eyes to see Rin's arm stretched forward. In her hand was Kim's pick, and the pick's blade stuck deep into the pit of his arm. He began to shake and twitch. He looked at his arm confused before seeing a small drop of the poison that had dripped from the blade onto his skin. Realizing what she had done he scoffed, dropped the sword, and threw her down hard. She landed on her back and grabbed at her chest taking several desperate huffs of air.

Crain held his forearm tightly and stared at the puncture in his arm as it leaked a brown colored mixture. He fell to a knee and started wheezing.

"Sorry, you left yourself wide open," Rin grunted standing to her feet.

She stepped over to him and kicked him in his mouth. He fell flat, face first onto the ground and his entire body began to tremble. She stood over him for a moment watching him suffer. She then crouched down and wiped the pick's blade clean on his pants leg. She then retracted the blade and tucked it at her waist. He cursed her under his breath in between a series of dry heaves and coughs.

"That poison's gonna work its way through you quick, you don't have the body mass to fight it for long," Rin said.

He began slowly crawling away from her. Each move made the next harder to make.

"You won't make it anywhere. The poison'll kill you eventually, and if the storm clouds pass the desert's heat'll kill you first." she looked up at a hawk circling them from above, "There's also the wildlife out here…"

She reached over and grabbed the sword he dropped. She looked directly into his eyes. He cut his at her and snarled. She returned the gaze with an even harsher one of her own.

"Let's see how much you enjoy being hunted down by animals," Rin said.

She raised the sword and stabbed it into the ground through his hand. He let out an agonizing yell as Rin stood and turned her back on him.

"Sorry about your father," she whispered over her shoulder.

She rushed over to where Kim was laying and collapsed at her side. She took one quick gaze at her wound and shivered.

"Kim?! Kim?!" she called gently shaking her.

Kim's eyes eventually rose up to her and she gently smiled.

Rin let out a sigh of relief, "Oh thank God."

She turned around and shouted over her shoulder, "Charlotte! Get up!"

Charlotte, while still conscious, couldn't move. She was in too much pain herself. Rin turned back to Kim and rubbed her arm.

"It's gonna be OK, we're gonna get you patched up alright?" Rin told her.

"I love you, Rin…. but no," Kim said.

Rin looked back at her confused.

"No what?"

"It's not gonna be OK…. *I'm* not gonna be OK."

"Don't say that," Rin begged her, "we can…"

"No…. no, you can't."

"Kim?" Rin cried.

"Listen to me," Kim said, her voice weak, "I'm done. I can't live like this anymore. Rin, I'm *so* tired. Not just from the six years in The Pool, but the four years I spent trying to put it all behind me, the six years I lived as an orphan feeling unloved and unwanted, and the five I spent spiraling after I lost my foster parents. I've lived an awful life Rin, and I'm so tired."

"But Kim…" tears began to fall from Rin's eyes.

"I've done so much wrong in my life, I've hurt so many people, and for what? To die in the middle of the desert with a hole in my body. What was it all for? What was my life for?"

"Kim! You're not gonna die here!" Rin assured her.

"Yes, I am…. I want to…. I need to."

The smile on her face grew a bit bigger.

"If God is real, I hope he lets me stand at the gates of heaven and just shout an apology through to everyone I sent there…. before he sends me to burn in hell," she laughed.

"Stop, that's not funny!" Rin shook her unamused.

"Rin, I am one of the worse things that ever happened to Joy City, nothing I did has ever meant anything for anyone, and the worst part is, I can't make that right. I'm a cancer to the city…. I need to die…"

"No, Kim stop!" Rin pleaded.

"Truthfully, the city, probably the world even, would just be a better place without me."

Rin buried her face in her knees as she began to cry.

"I deserve this Rin, I do. All the bad I did in my life, this is my atonement, for every person I…"

"But what about Cindy?! What about me and LuLu and Blake?!" Rin cried, her face now bright red and stained with tears.

"Y'all are gonna be fine, I know y'all will, I just hate I couldn't keep my promise to Mom and Dad."

Pain and death hadn't struck fear in Kim's heart in nearly a decade, and didn't even now. What truly hurt her was her failure to keep the promise she made to their parents. While she truly believed Rin could take care of herself, in her mind she had failed both her and their parents.

Rin fell onto Kim's body hugging her tight, crying onto her shoulder.

"Kim, please, I need you, please, I can't lose you too, please!" she sobbed.

"You made it twenty-six years without me," she smiled, "you'll be OK, I know you will."

"Kim no…. please…" Rin continued weeping.

Kim took a deep breath that ended in another sickly cough.

"I love you Rin. Happy Birthday. Tell everyone I love them, and tell them all I said thank you for being the angels they were in my life."

She took one last breath before she fell silent and still. Rin cried as her sister faded away in her arms.

Chapter 9

Family IIII

It was a quiet morning in Joy City, a rare but favorable one. There was a light breeze about the air that chilled the city as the sun's rays beat down on it from above. Light friendly chatter ensued from people passing by each other on the city's streets; nothing unruly, no scenes being made. There were children on summer break playing basketball on the old courts or games of kickball in the park's open fields. The city's aura just felt good, as good as the aura in Joy City could feel. It was still considered a crime haven, most born inside still desired a way out, but the days of it feeling hellish to even exist in seemed to have passed, at least for some. The day was calm. These were the types of days the city seemed to lack for so long, the types of days it needed.

Rin sat in the grass hugging her knees. She gently rocked back and forth as her eyes moved slowly from left to right. There was a lump in her throat. She was trying to speak but found it difficult.

She just couldn't quite find the words she wanted to speak. Every sentence that passed through her head was hopelessly crushed before it ever had a chance to leave her mouth.

In front of her rested two matching stone monuments. Both showing their age having been eroded and weather beaten for over a thousand days and nights. She looked around, ensuring she was alone. She took a deep breath that ended in a shiver.

"Hey," she began, "it's me again."

A forced grin came across her face.

"Don't have a lot of time this morning but I was driving by on the way back to the house and just figured.... a quick stop wouldn't hurt. I'll try to keep it together this time," she lightly laughed.

She took another deep breath before continuing.

"I was thinking the other day, I never really apologized to y'all for everything I kept from you, everything I did, everything I was doing. There was a lot going on and I also had a hole in my leg at the time but.... I was raised better than that, I should've been better. I'm sorry.... sometimes I really feel like everything was my fault. I'm sure there's a million ways to spin it but I always end up feeling like the things I did or didn't do are the reason I'm sitting here talking to you like this."

She turned her head to the right away from the stones. Even after several years it still hurt to look directly at them.

"I think what drove me to make the decisions that I made was a lack of support, emotional I mean.

241

And at the time y'all were in no condition health wise to provide that. So I don't blame you. I needed help, a sound mind, a voice to tell me, 'No Rin, you shouldn't do that, you can't do that', and I didn't really get that until…"

She turned her head back towards the matching stones but her eyes continued left until another stone came into her line of sight. Matching in size and shape the only difference was the wear upon it, just two weeks to the others' many.

"…. until I found you, but by that time it was too late."

She stared at the tombstone for a moment in disbelief. Not a single day of the past fortnight made the sight any easier to digest.

"If someone would've told me years ago that one day I'd be the surviving one of the four of us, I wouldn't have believed them. I don't know why. I mean, it makes sense, I *am* the youngest technically. Maybe it was the timing, maybe I just thought we'd have more time with each other? The last Christmas we spent together…. the *only* Christmas we all spent together, I thought our happiest days were ahead of us…"

She shook her head.

"… but nope, not us. Happiness always seems to find a way to evade us. Why? I don't know. Maybe we're cursed? I hate to sound negative but just thinking about everything that's happened to us over the past thirty years, we gotta be cursed."

She picked a blade of grass from in front of her and tossed it into the air. The breeze caught it and instantly whisked it away. She looked back towards the cleaner of the three stones and smiled a little.

"Cindy leaves today. She's done really well with everything. Better than me actually," she laughed, "I'm so bad at reading people though, so I'm not sure if it's all just a front, but we talked and I think she's gonna be OK. Actually…. I promise she will be. I'll make sure of that. You showed me how to support someone you love through loss, so you have my word, she'll be OK, I promise."

Rin pushed herself up onto her feet and brushed some stray blades of grass off her pants.

"I know y'all are probably tired of hearing my voice by now." she giggled, "Tired of listening to me crying all day long. I'll try to start puttin some days in between visits, let y'all rest."

She stepped in front of the tombstone farthest to the right and placed her hand on it.

"I love you guys…"

She began walking to her left. As she passed by each stone, she drug her fingers across their tops.

"Bye Mom…. bye Dad…. bye Kim," she whispered.

~

Rin splashed some water on her face before turning the faucet off. She tried to shake her hands dry before eventually just wiping them on her pants leg. She looked in the mirror and frowned. She looked a mess. She had bags under her eyes, her face was still a bit red from crying on the way home, and her hair hadn't been brushed in days. Though she didn't like what she saw, she looked far better than she had the day before. It was a process, but she was healing.

She was exhausted and if she could have she would have just flopped back down onto her bed and slept the rest of the day away. However, she had a house full of guests and someone to see off in a few moments. She took a few seconds to compose herself and walked out of the guest room of Kim's house.

She decided to stay at the house until Cindy left town to help Lei-Ling move into her new apartment. She knew she needed to be wherever Cindy was and figured Kim's house would be more comfortable for Cindy than her own. As she made her way down the hallway, she passed by Kim's room. She could feel her presence, as if she could possibly be inside lying in her bed. The thought sent a shiver down her spine. She started down the stairs and froze midway as she heard the doorbell sound.

"Was that the TV?" a voice from the kitchen asked.

"No, that was the door," another answered.

"I got it," Rin called continuing down the steps.

She got to the door and pulled it open. In front of her stood two men she recognized but couldn't immediately name. One was tall, thin, and dark skinned. In his hand he held a bouquet of flowers. The other, holding a card, was fair skinned, a bit lanky, and freckle faced.

"Hey Rin?" the man holding the flowers spoke.

"Hey…" she answered still trying to put names to their faces.

"I don't know if you remember us, we used to work with Kim years ago at…"

"Oh oh oh, yeah. Will and Max, right? We all spent New Year's together a couple years ago?" she said palming her forehead.

"Yeah," they nodded in unison.

"Yeah, of course I remember you guys, I just…. I'm sorry, I've just had so much on my mind lately with…"

"Oh no worries," William said.

"We understand," Max added.

William gulped hard before speaking again.

"Ummm…. we were…. real sorry to hear about Kim," he eased out.

"Yeah…" Rin breathed looking down.

"She was our work buddy for a lot of years, that place wasn't the same after she left," Max said.

"Yeah, I bet," Rin smiled.

William held out the bouquet of flowers he was holding; a cluster of white roses. Max held out the card.

"Well, we wanted to bring these by, say our condolences. Did y'all already have a funeral?" William asked.

Rin took the flowers and card in her arms.

"Uhhh no, she was ummm…. not that keen on the thought of having a bunch of people look down at her in a casket. She always told me if she was to go before me not to have a funeral, just a private burial service for the family and to keep the day rolling."

William grinned, "That sounds like her, she always hated being the center of attention."

"Yeah," Rin sighed, "but if you guys wanna.... visit her.... she's right next to our parents."

William nodded, "OK, yeah we'll definitely stop by today."

Rin smiled and nodded.

"Well, thank you for the flowers, they're beautiful, and the card as well. I appreciate it."

"Of course, no problem," Max said.

"Hey, anything you need, both our numbers are on the card. We loved Kim like she was family, so anything you need, we're both just outside of Joy City, the drive is nothin, don't ever hesitate to reach out."

"Gotcha," Rin nodded, "thanks fellas."

"We'll be in touch. Take it easy," William added.

"I will, drive safe."

Rin watched as they left. Their visit warmed her heart. It made her happy knowing that despite everything, despite how she thought of herself, the few people Kim kept close all loved her and thought her a special person. She smelled the flowers and smiled.

She spun around and shut the door behind her with her foot. She walked into the kitchen and was met by several sets of eyes. LuLu and Blake sat at the kitchen table, Ms. C stood over the sink washing dishes, and Charlotte and Terrance in separate corners leaning against the wall with their arms folded across their chests.

"More flowers?" LuLu asked.

"And a card," Rin said, "from her old work friends William and Max."

She set the flowers and card down on the table next to LuLu.

"Did you get addresses from them so we can start working on the thank-you letters?" LuLu asked.

Rin froze realizing it had slipped her mind.

"Ugh, nope, but it's fine, both their numbers are on the card," Rin said.

"Alright, any more been delivered?"

"Yeah, yesterday actually."

LuLu grabbed a pen and notepad resting in the middle of the table. She opened the pad up to a clean page and looked up at Rin.

"A bouquet of daisies from someone named Tony?" Rin said, "There was no address on the tag though."

"I think I know who that is," LuLu said, "Kim's foster parents and his use to be close. I think his family owns a car dealership downtown. I can find the address online. Who else?"

"Some red carnations from a Paul?"

"Owns a diner downtown we use to go to as kids, got him," she said scribbling on the notepad, "who else?"

"Ummm…. a bunch of gardenias. The tag said Leonard, Diane, and Kim?"

"*And Kim?*" LuLu asked.

"I know who that is." Ms. C turned around, "A couple who adopted from Little Angels about four years ago. They adopted a little girl named Kim.

Your sister took a real liking to her and actually used to watch her from time to time when her parents wanted a night out to themselves."

Rin recalled Kim mentioning babysitting for some friends from time to time. She always assumed she was just lying to cover up the secret boyfriend she swore she was hiding from everyone.

"Can you get me their address or a number I can reach them at?" LuLu asked.

"Of course," Ms. C nodded.

"OK, anyone else?" LuLu asked turning back to Rin.

She thought for a moment.

"Oh yeah…. like nine roses."

"*Nine* roses?" LuLu asked raising an eyebrow.

"Yeah, but they were different colors. It was four red roses and five white ones, they were all in the same bouquet though."

"Four red and five white? Was there a name tag?" LuLu asked.

"Yeah, it just said Angel."

Charlotte and Terrance's heads suddenly lifted and turned towards each other. They made brief eye contact before looking away.

"Angel?" LuLu repeated looking around at everyone.

Blake and Ms. C both shrugged.

"Yeah, I don't know who it could be and they didn't leave an address. I guess we'll just have to put a thank you up in the air tonight for them," Rin said.

Terrance cut his eyes in Charlotte's direction. She responded with a discreet shaking of her head.

The sound of footsteps on the staircase pulled everyone's attention. Cindy, wearing a backpack and carrying a small duffel bag on her shoulder came rushing down. She rounded the corner and poked her head into the kitchen.

"Lei-Ling's outside," she announced to them.

"Hold on." Ms. C quickly dried her hands off on a towel and walked over to where Cindy stood. "I wanna meet her, make sure she's not tryin to steal you away from us."

Cindy lightly smiled. LuLu and Blake stood from the table and walked over towards her as well.

"You got everything?" Blake asked her.

"Yeah, it's just these two bags. I didn't pack much," she told him.

The four of them headed outside. Rin looked to Charlotte still leaning against the wall in the corner.

"You can go on and head out there, I'mma put these flowers with the rest, I'll be out in a minute."

Charlotte nodded. She looked to Terrance and silently motioned for him to follow. The two of them made their way outside. Rin walked into the living room and placed the flowers and card on the coffee table with the other dozens they had received over the past two weeks. Some had already begun to dry out and crumble but she still found the arrangement of them all so beautiful. She took a step back and looked over the table. The varying colors and shapes of the flowers popping out from the green foliage they rested upon brought a smile to her face. The several heartfelt cards lined around the edge of the table were also a pleasing sight.

She backed out the room and rounded the corner into the kitchen. She came to a pause as she passed by the refrigerator. On it she saw the photo of Kim, herself, and their parents she had placed there years ago. Next to it though was a photo of Kim she had never seen before. In it Kim was posing looking back over her shoulder. She stood in front of what appeared to be a very old building. She couldn't name it but she felt like she recognized the building's brickwork, something about it was familiar. Towards the bottom of the photo, she could see a narrow path leading to a door with a long rectangular window pane. Both sides of the path were lined with weeds growing wild in every direction. Even the pathway and door looked familiar. She felt like she had been there before.

Unable to place the location, her focus moved to Kim. She looked a bit younger than she was when they first met; a bit skinnier as well. Though what truly struck her was the enormous smile on her face. Not only was it the biggest smile she had ever seen on Kim, but it was the biggest smile she had ever seen on anyone in her life. In her eyes was a joy she couldn't even begin to put into words. To Rin, it was the most beautiful photo she had ever seen of her sister. So beautiful, it made her wish they had held a funeral for her. The photo would have been a perfect obituary cover.

"I love that picture of her."

Rin turned her head around and saw LuLu peeking from around the corner.

"I took it actually." she added, "Got it

developed and just forgot to ever give it to her. I stuck it on my fridge and it's just been there for years, thought you might want it."

Rin turned back around and continued to study the photo.

"She looks so…. happy," Rin said.

"She was. That was outside of Little Angels, it was taken the day she adopted Cindy."

The familiarity of the photo's location immediately made sense. Kim had taken Rin up to Little Angels a couple of times since she had moved to Joy City.

"Never seen her smile like that," Rin said.

"Yeah, me either, a day before or after," LuLu said.

Rin couldn't look away, something about the photo was mesmerizing to her. LuLu took a few steps forward until she was standing right behind her.

"When this was taken…. she had already been involved with that…. Pool thing for about a year. When I realized that, it puzzled me at first. Like why would she wanna bring a child into her life with everything she had goin on? But then I thought about it and I think for her it was her relief, her claim to still being a good person. I can't even imagine how dark of a place she had to have been in when she started doing what she was doing, but I think Cindy was what kept her sane during it all. The love of that mother-daughter relationship and the sister-like relationship it eventually matured into, she needed it. No one realized it at the time because, well, no one knew what she had going on behind the scenes, but really, she needed Cindy just as much, maybe even more than Cindy needed her."

The thought sent chills down Rin's spine. A person being so mentally and emotionally broken, so desperately in need of love. It stung thinking about how lonely Kim must have felt in the years following her foster parents' deaths.

"She looks so young," Rin whispered.

"Yeah, that was almost ten years ago I think, y'all would've been about twenty, twenty-one maybe."

Rin began to recall where she was in life at twenty years old. She remembered waking up at the crack of dawn to finish whatever school assignment she failed to complete the night before, then struggle to make it through the school day without falling asleep or having a panic attack in the middle of class, to then spend hours waiting tables to make minimum wage just to get off, go home, and do more school work that she would eventually fall asleep trying to complete. She would repeat this cycle every day while still managing to find time to check in with her sickly parents to ensure they were alright, of which the majority of the time they weren't. Meanwhile, Kim was in a lonely depression, sitting on her foster parents' millions, making hundreds of thousands in The Pool, smiling as she went to adopt her daughter. Some pair of twins they were.

"Thank you," Rin whispered to her.

LuLu smiled and nodded. She stared at the photo alongside Rin and sighed.

"God, I can't believe she's…"

"Girls, come on!" Ms. C yelled from the door, "Cindy's gotta get going!"

"We're comin!" LuLu called back.

She grabbed Rin's shoulder and gently tore her away from the photo. They headed outside where everyone was gathered around Lei-Ling's car.

"Hi Ms. Rin," Lei-Ling's eyes lit up as she greeted her.

"Hi sweetheart," Rin smiled hugging her.

Blake stuffed Cindy's two bags into the trunk and slammed it shut.

"Alright, y'all are set," he said.

Cindy began making her way around giving everyone a hug goodbye. Each embrace was followed by a forced sympathetic smile. She saved Rin for last. Their eyes locked and Cindy fell hard into her chest giving her the longest and tightest squeeze. Rin kissed the top of her head and rubbed her back.

"I love you sweetheart," Rin whispered to her.

"Love you too," she whispered back.

The tremble in her voice nearly caused Rin to burst into tears.

"Anything you need baby, call me OK? Anything at all," Rin said.

"Yep," she responded.

They would've said more but, truthfully, they had talked enough over the past two weeks. There wasn't much left they could say to each other. They pulled back and Rin kissed her on her cheek.

"Let me know when y'all get there OK?"

"Alright, I will," she said opening the car door.

"Nice to meet you all," Lei-Ling smiled as she

walked around to the driver's side of the car.

They all responded echoing her sentiments.

"You girls drive safe," Ms. C said.

"Yes ma'am, we will," Lei-Ling answered as she ducked into the car.

The car started up and in an instant, Cindy and Lei-Ling were gone, leaving them all standing on the lawn in silence.

"Ugh…. bless her heart," Ms. C whined, "I know she's so torn up right now. I just hope…"

"No," Rin interrupted, "she's fine. We talked, she's hurt, but she's fine, she's OK…. she is."

"What about you though?" Charlotte stepped behind her and placed a hand on her shoulder, "Are you alright?"

She began to pout but tried to hide it biting down on her lip. She closed her eyes and began to shake. She looked over her shoulder at Charlotte.

"If I said no, would it change anything?" she murmured.

Charlotte wrapped her arms tightly around Rin, locking her hands over her chest. LuLu joined in hugging her from the side as the others huddled around her.

~

Rin sat at the kitchen table halfway asleep. The sound of Charlotte washing dishes was the only thing keeping her awake. After breakfast and Cindy's departure back to her school, the others stayed to comfort her and ended up staying for dinner as well.

254

While everyone else eventually left Charlotte stayed behind to help Rin clean up.

"Alright, dishes are done…"

Charlotte turned around and froze at the sight of Rin staring off into space. She looked dazed, like she was struggling to even keep her head up.
Charlotte walked over and waved her hand in front of her face.

"Hey, you good?" she asked.

Rin snapped from her trance and looked up at her.

"Yeah…. yeah, what's up?"

"Dishes are done," Charlotte repeated.

"Oh…. thanks, I appreciate it," she said yawning.

A brief moment of silence came between them as Charlotte looked at her concerned, as Rin stared back confused.

"What?" she asked.

As if the single word was her begging Charlotte for a talk, she pulled a chair out from the table and sat down.

"Talk to me," Charlotte said.

"About what?" Rin asked.

Charlotte shot her an impatient glare.

"I'm just tired, it was a long day. I just need some sleep," Rin assured her.

"Nah, I know you better than that. When you're tired you just go straight to sleep, you don't just sit there lookin punch drunk."

"I'm just tired," she repeated, "between cooking breakfast, dinner, and tryin to hold myself together emotionally, I'm just drained."

"Well, you pulled it off, dinner was kinda late, food was a bit cold but you know, you tried…"

A rare attempt at humor from Charlotte. Rin cut her eyes at her.

"I'm just messin with you," she smiled, nudging her leg under the table, "everything was fine, everyone had a good time."

"Yeah, I guess. Terrance left kinda early though," Rin pointed out.

A look of disgust came over Charlotte's face at the mention of his name.

"I'm surprised you even invited him today, more surprised he actually showed up," she said.

Rin raised an eyebrow at her comment.

"What do you mean? Why wouldn't I invite him?"

Charlotte looked equally surprised by her answer.

"I mean…. am I wrong for thinking all of this was kinda his fault?" she shrugged.

"No," she sighed, "you're not wrong, but I actually don't blame him. I don't even really know why I don't but I don't. Maybe he just spun the story really nice and I fell for it."

"What story?"

"He didn't tell you anything?" Rin asked surprised.

Charlotte leaned back into her chair and shook her head no.

"Me and him haven't had too much to say to each other since all this."

"Oh…. I see. Well, everything the guy told us out there Terrance pretty much confirmed. His father did wanna end The Pool after Kim's foster parents were killed and everyone but Terrance was in favor. He said he was just so emotionally messed up after losing his best friend he just kinda felt like The Pool, and of course Kim, were all he had left and he didn't wanna lose that too."

Charlotte buried her face in her hands. She peeked through the space between her fingers at Rin.

"Oh my god," she moaned, "please don't tell me you fell for that garbage."

"I mean, it makes sense," Rin shrugged. "I've been there, so messed up in the head you just start makin a bunch of poor decisions. It happens."

Charlotte shook her head, disappointed in Rin for what she felt was her being naïve.

"OK, whatever I guess. What else did he say?"

"So, the guy did walk and threaten to expose The Pool and so Terrance did pay some gang members to kill him that night."

"Wow…" Charlotte whispered in disbelief.

"Yeah, I know, there's no justification for that one at all. But anyway, everyone left after that. He said he never heard from any of them ever again except for that Rose woman. He said the guy's dad and her were basically lovers at the time and so of course she didn't appreciate what he did. He called her and tried to plead his case but she wouldn't hear it."

"Wha-plead his case?" Charlotte was stunned by her word choice.

"That's what he said, I don't know," Rin said holding her hands up, "He asked her about his son, who was about eighteen at the time, but she said he disappeared and she hadn't seen or heard from him. Now, that's the part that doesn't quite add up. In the desert he said she took him in, but Terrance remembers her saying she hadn't seen or heard from him."

"Maybe she found him later?" Charlotte suggested.

"Maybe?" Rin shrugged, "But I'm almost thinking she just didn't want Terrance to know that she had taken him in. If the father and her were lovers she was probably pretty close to his son too, probably looked at him like he was her own. After what he did, she probably just didn't want Terrance to have any contact with him ever again. Probably just wanted to move on and put the whole thing behind them. Plus, initially she lied to him about what happened to his father, a talk with Terrance might've exposed the truth."

"Makes sense."

"Yeah, and so they did move on, and for ten years they lived their lives, she never talked to Terrance ever again, she had probably almost completely forgotten that The Pool ever even existed, and then…"

"Then you showed up in Joy City and put every bad memory she was trying to suppress on the local news."

"Unreal right?" Rin bit her lip.

"Tsk…"

"She told him what really happened all those years ago and shortly after that they had revenge on their minds."

"OK, that answers some questions but how were they finding us the way they were?"

"I mean, these aren't just gangbangers. They were all once assassins too, tracking us down was probably the easiest part for them."

"OK OK, well, what about the day we showed up at Terrance's house. Why didn't he warn us about all this then?"

"If I had to guess, for one, he had some skeletons in his closet he probably wanted to keep hidden. That, and after all this time he probably had just forgotten about it. I mean the three recordings we played him didn't actually mention him at all, plus that happened like fifteen years ago? He probably just assumed everyone had moved on from that, some of them actually moved out of Joy City, some out the country. That's where they got all those crazy weapons they had. That stuff didn't come from here, that stuff was forged overseas. And then the kid, well.... he just never suspected the kid at all."

Charlotte fell back into her chair and crossed her arms still unsatisfied.

".... I can't believe him," she mumbled under her breath.

"He's not such a bad guy, he's just a product of this city. I appreciate him comin to me and comin clean like that, he didn't have to, but he did."

"Wait, you didn't ask, he just told you all this himself?"

"Yeah, he just showed up at the door one day last week. I don't know, I guess maybe he felt like he owed me an explanation?"

"Still…" Charlotte sucked her teeth.

"You're pretty mad at him huh?"

"Mad ain't the word."

Rin sighed.

"I guess I'm not because, well…. I know he's havin to deal with this too. He didn't get away scot free, he's suffering just like we are, but I get it though."

Rin noticed Charlotte slouch down in her chair a bit. Her lip began to quiver and she blew air out her nose.

"I remember the day we went to talk to Pedro's family to tell them what happened to him all those years ago. That was one of the hardest things I've ever had to do, and Terrance did all the talking, we were really just there. After we walked out that house I told myself never again. I couldn't sit in front of another family and explain to them why their son, daughter, brother, sister, or whatever is gone because of something so illicit we can't even afford to tell them everything they deserve to know. Sitting in front of his family was hard, but sitting in front of Aaliyah's last week…. I've never seen people cry like that before."

She wiped a few tears forming in the corners of her eyes.

"I'm the only one left. Pedro, Aaliyah, Kim, they were like family, and they're all gone," her voice was breaking, "and he has the nerve to give you that garbage excuse…"

"Hey hey, it's OK. I know, the whole situation is completely busted, I just don't wanna go pointing fingers. And trust me I know the feeling of having to break that kinda news to someone. Telling LuLu about Kim was rough, telling Blake was rough, but Ms. C…" Rin shivered, "…. for a moment I thought I killed that woman."

"Awww yeah, she basically raised her huh? That had to be hard on her."

Rin sighed shaking her head.

"The woman literally collapsed to the floor in tears. It was bad. I've never seen anyone break down like that before in my life."

"Sheesh, did you actually tell her the details?"

"No, of course not, that literally might have taken her out. I just left it at she got caught in the crossfire of somethin, wrong place wrong time."

"What about Cindy?" Charlotte asked.

"I drove up there to her school to tell her in person and well…. it went about as well as you would expect."

Charlotte nodded behind a sorrowing expression.

"She'll be OK though," Rin said, "she's a really strong mentally tough kid. It cut her deep for sure, but she's gonna be fine."

Rin wasn't sure if she actually knew this or if she had just fooled herself into believing it because it was easier to deal with. She wanted to believe it of course but aside from Cindy telling her she was OK there was no real proof to her claim that she was or would be. She hoped she was right though, she really needed herself to be right.

Rin ended up staring at the light fixture above her head as her mind wandered. So many things playing back in her head, so many conversations, thoughts, and feelings spinning about inside her brain.

"Hey?" Charlotte's voice brought her attention back down, "You thinkin pretty hard over there, what's up?"

"Just everything," Rin shrugged, "There's just a lot on my mind right now. This week's been especially crazy tryin to get everything settled with her estate."

"She had a will didn't she. Doesn't all that almost take care of itself?"

"She *had* a will," Rin corrected her, "but when I showed up, she tore it up and never got to fully revising it, but she did at some point make me power of attorney over the estate in case of her…. untimely death. She told me a while ago how she wanted everything divvied up, but without a will, there's just no easy way to settle an estate as enormous as hers. There's a lot of deep process verification, ID matching, and it's just all been one massive headache."

"*ID matching*? Is it that serious? How big is the estate?" Charlotte asked.

"Ummm…." Rin scratched her head as she calculated in her mind, "about eight million liquidated, about one hundred twenty-eight million in hard assets…"

"Whoa what?! A hundred and twenty-eight million?! What the hell was she into?!"

"Real estate mostly. She owned a lot of land."

"No way," Charlotte shook her head, "how did she manage to find a hundred and twenty-eight million dollars' worth of real estate in Joy City?"

"She didn't, the only thing she ever owned in Joy City was this house and whatever car she was driving at the time. But the northern part of the state, where all the money is, her name is on a lot of property up there worth a lot of money. Her foster parents made a lot from The Pool, they pocketed somewhere around two million and grew that with some smart investments. She was their only heir, so when they were killed, they left her everything, every penny. Luckily, before that, they taught her how to make money, how to flip checks, how to turn a five-figure payout into a seven-figure profit. She listened. As much as she despised money and the things it drove people to do, she was very good at making it. She took the millions her foster parents left her and added over a hundred million more to it by herself, no partners, no financial advisors, nothin."

"Sheesh, and I thought I was doin somethin with the gym. I just barely cracked twenty mil last year."

"Hmmm, I figured she would've shared what she knew with the rest of y'all?"

"Ehhh.... nah. None of us really talked about money like that, it was sorta taboo. One of the unspoken rules of The Pool, don't count anyone else's pockets. We were all gettin paid about the same for the same kind of work so what you did with what you made was no one else's business."

"Makes sense."

"So wait, you and Cindy are splittin a hundred and twenty-eight million down the middle?"

"No, she had eight million liquidated spread across a few different bank accounts that we can go spend tomorrow if we want to. She's also got a duffle bag upstairs with a couple hundred thousand in cash in it but all that's completely separate from the hundred twenty-eight. That hundred twenty-eight is in hard assets, property for the most part. If we want the money, we can get it, but we'd have to sell those assets, but in keeping them they'll pay us both for the rest of our lives, so selling them just doesn't really make sense. Right now, from all those assets combined she has nearly a hundred thousand dollars rollin in every month."

"Geez, chica was cleanin up."

"Yeah, but splitting it all up is where it gets kinda tricky. By her own wishes her entire estate is to be split seventy-thirty. Me and Cindy split the seventy percent, plus everything liquidated, and the other thirty percent is split three ways between LuLu, Blake, and Ms. C. The way the math works out me and Cindy would get roughly forty million each, and LuLu, Blake, and Ms. C about thirteen million each."

"She made sure everyone she loved was taken care of, that's awesome. Hard to even believe somethin like that comin from someone born and raised here."

Rin kicked back in her chair and began staring

up at the light fixture again.

"Kim was living with a lot of irreparable guilt. She wasn't proud of the things she did while she was in The Pool, she hated herself for it actually, it haunted her every day. Her release, or what allowed her to forgive and convince herself that she wasn't a horrible person was philanthropy. In the two years I lived with her she was charitable beyond reason. It made her happy to give back some of the fortune she made from The Pool, but still it was never enough to fully curb the guilt and shame she was suffering from. About two years ago she told me when she left this Earth she wanted every cent she owned to be used first to take care of the people she loved, and second to make a difference in the lives of kids in Joy City who were dealt tough hands like her."

"That's why she's givin Ms. C thirteen," Charlotte said.

Rin nodded.

"She knew that woman's heart, before she touches a penny of it for herself, she's gonna take care of those kids at Little Angels first."

"Man..." Charlotte smiled.

"She wanted to feel like everything she did in her life was for something. She knew there was no moral justification for what she was doing, what she did, but every life she took, every life her foster parents took, for every dollar made from those lives to go back into something that mattered, something good, she felt she owed Joy City that for all the terror she and The Pool brought upon it."

Charlotte's smile quickly faded as she

considered Rin's words.

"I guess…. I guess I never thought of it that way. We really didn't do much to help pull the city's name out the mud huh?"

"It's not your fault, this city just really has the worst effect on the people living inside it. I didn't believe it at first but living here these past four years, I see it now, there's no way not to."

They sat silently for a moment thinking to themselves until Charlotte broke the silence giggling to herself.

"What?" Rin asked.

"I'm just thinkin, what on earth is a foster home gonna do with thirteen million dollars?" she laughed.

"What on earth am *I* gonna do with forty million dollars?" Rin responded.

"Tsk…. whatever you want." Charlotte smirked, "What do you wanna do?"

Rin placed her hand over her mouth and thought for a moment. She looked all around the kitchen until her eyes finally stopped on Charlotte.

"Well for starters, move."

"Move?" Charlotte raised an eyebrow.

Rin nodded.

"I talked to Cindy, one of the last conversations she had with Kim, they talked about her moving out of Joy City."

"Yeah?"

"Yeah, this city just hasn't been kind to our family in the past thirty years and I'm not really tryin to stick around to see what else it has for us."

"Where you gonna go?"

"I don't know yet," she shrugged.

"Anywhere but here huh?"

"Pretty much, once everything with the estate gets settled, I'll have to sit down with her and we'll figure it out."

"What are you gonna do with the house?"

"I'mma let Cindy make that call. I feel like she's more entitled to it than I am. If she wants to sell it, we'll sell it, if not then I don't know. She seemed pretty adamant about gettin out of Joy City for good, so I can't imagine she'd wanna keep it especially if she's not gonna be living in it."

"OK, what about that super car sitting in the driveway?"

"I don't know. It's a hundred-thousand-dollar car with no tags or registration. I'm not even sure what we can do with it legally. But I don't want it, it's too flashy for me so I guess if Cindy wants it, it's hers too."

"Girl isn't even twenty years old yet and she's already got forty million dollars and a hundred-thousand-dollar car," Charlotte said.

Rin laughed.

"Yeah, the cold part is though, she doesn't even care. She doesn't care about the money, the car, and I doubt she cares about this house either. She just wants me and everyone she loves out of Joy City."

"I don't blame her. Honestly, I been feelin that way for a while too. Growing up my dad used to always say, 'Joy City is undefeated', no one's ever beaten it, not while livin inside it. I didn't always know what he meant by it but as I got older and saw the city for what it really was, I started to get it. This place is like a black hole, you can't stay here and live the life you want."

"What made you stay this long?"

"The Pool for the longest, family of course, and then the gym happened, but now no Pool, no gym, and I could probably convince the family to roll with me wherever so..."

"Speaking of the gym, what's up with that? You gonna rebuild it?" Rin asked.

"I don't know yet. If I do definitely won't be here though."

Rin suddenly began smiling at her from across the table. Charlotte took notice of her quick change of expression and drew back a bit.

"Wh-what?" she asked confused.

"Move with me," Rin said with a smile.

"What?"

"Move with me. C'mon, let's get outta Joy City?"

"Like…. like together?"

"Yeah?"

Charlotte shrunk and began to blush as a worried look came over her face.

"Uhhh…. Rin you know I'm not…. you know…"

Rin's face immediately turned realizing where she was getting at. She rolled her eyes at her implication.

"Oh my god Charlotte, no, not like that," Rin said.

".... oh," Charlotte looked away now blushing even more.

"Geez, don't flatter yourself, you're cute, but if I was gonna swing that way I feel like I could do better."

Charlotte sucked her teeth at her jab.

"Just come with me, whatever city I end up moving to just find you a place out there too. It won't be far, just like you said, anywhere but here. You could rebuild the gym there too," Rin explained.

"Sounds like you just want some job security when you move," she smirked.

"Oh no," Rin laughed, "my sister just left me forty million, trust I'm not workin for anyone ever again. Speaking of, I don't remember if I told you this or not yet, but I quit."

"Funny," Charlotte twisted her lips.

"Hey, I'm serious though, move with me. We can rebuild it together, bigger and better than it was."

"I mean..." Charlotte began.

"C'mon," Rin whined, "look, I'll be honest, the real reason I want you to come is cause really, besides Cindy, who's still gonna be in school anyway, it's not like I have any other friends or family to bring with me. And you said it, the city's undefeated, what are we even still doing here, hasn't it already taken enough from us?"

Charlotte thought hard for a moment. Her face told Rin she was considering it.

"You got time," Rin added, "until I get her estate settled and figure out what we're gonna do with the house. I probably won't even be able to move until like the end of the year, if even by then. But just think about it, OK?"

"Alright," Charlotte nodded.

Rin fell back into her chair with a content grin. She took a deep breath and closed her eyes. She looked prepared to fall asleep right there at the table.

"You look like you still got somthin else on your mind," Charlotte said.

Rin opened her eyes and shrugged.

"It's just crazy, everything that's happened you know? It just all feels like one bad dream."

Charlotte huffed and nodded in agreement.

"Hey," Rin crossed her arms over her chest, "you ever wonder how the city got like this? I mean even before the gang raids it wasn't necessarily people's favorite place to visit then either right?"

"Honestly, no, I never put that much thought into it. The city being as bad as it is has always benefited me and whatever I was doin at the time, so I never questioned it. Like I said it's just a black hole, sucks you up and spits you back out, usually worse off. No one's ever made it out clean, some don't make it out at all. Why? Why this place? I don't really know. But if I had to guess I'd say the city was just unlucky. Fate picked it to be what it is, and it's simply…"

"… Joy City," Rin finished her sentence, "the place where you don't write your own story, you *are* the story, a tiny piece of one anyway."

"Mhmmm…. the place where everyone lives by the three unspoken rules, live with somebody worth dyin for, get some money, and stay out the way….

Joy City," Charlotte sighed.

Rin closed her eyes, sighed, and bowed her head, ".... yep, Joy City."

Chapter 10

The Epilogue

Rin woke in the middle of the night to a horrible headache. She rolled over in her bed and glanced at the alarm clock on the nightstand.

"12:34," it read.

She groaned as she rolled back over and sandwiched her head in between her pillow. She hoped the pressure would relieve some of the pain but it only seemed to get worse. The pain was so sharp, falling back asleep seemed impossible. She tossed and turned under her sheets and cover for a while but then eventually began getting hot. She could feel her shirt becoming damp, sticking to her skin as she began to sweat. She tossed the sheets and cover down to the foot of the bed and tried to ignore both the heat and her head pain; neither subsided.

She eventually propped herself up on her elbow and felt the bed sheet beneath her; it was soaked. She rolled out of bed onto her feet and almost toppled over trying to take a step. For a moment the room appeared to be spinning. She began to worry.

Her heart started beating faster and the air around her began to feel unbreathable. She braced herself up against the doorframe leading to the bathroom and held on until she was able to calm herself down through a series of deep breaths.

She reached inside the bathroom and flicked on the light. The light hit her eyes and she immediately turned away. The brightness caused another small spike of pain in her head. She slowly eased into the bathroom and leaned over the vanity. She placed her hands down flat around the sink and stared at herself in the mirror. Her face was red and a bit damp. She turned on the faucet and splashed some cold water onto her face that helped her begin to cool down. The pain in her head began easing and she could now feel the cool air shooting down on her from the air vent above.

She dried her face with a towel hanging on the back of the door and began wondering what she had just experienced. She simply wrote it off as a panic attack, something she was no stranger to, especially as of recent.

Interrupting her thought, from her stomach came a loud rumbling sound. She looked down at it and remembered in the midst of cooking, hosting a house full of guests, and trying to keep her emotions in check that she hadn't actually eaten yesterday. In fact, she couldn't remember having had so much as a glass of water. She assumed her body could've also just been reacting to feeling dehydrated and starved. Not to mention the immense amount of stress weighing on her.

On the side of the sink rested Kim's hair pick. Rin tied her hair into a messy bun on top of her head and stuck the pick's teeth into it holding it in place. She left the bathroom, passed through the bedroom, and stepped out into the hallway.

Charlotte didn't leave until late, so Rin ended up staying at Kim's house for the night. She walked down the hall and shivered as she passed by the door to Kim's room. She had been avoiding stepping inside the room for two weeks but knew eventually she would have no choice but to step inside to begin cleaning it out. The thought of it terrified her, though she wasn't completely sure why. She didn't know if she was afraid of what she might find or just the thought of being in a place she spent so much time in. She remembered Kim's unmade bed the last time she peeked inside the room. *What if it still smells like her,* she thought.

She passed by the room and headed downstairs and into the kitchen. Flicking on the light, she silently praised Charlotte as she saw the sink empty of dishes. Her stomach loudly growled again. She remembered having stuffed some leftovers in the refrigerator yesterday, but her mouth was so dry she desperately needed something to drink first. She remembered whenever Kim was stressed, tired, overwhelmed, or anything of the sort, she always made herself a glass of tea. At the moment she felt she was all of the above and more.

She walked over to the cabinet and swung it open. She looked and noticed Charlotte had placed the drinking glasses higher than where Kim normally kept them. She had to step up on her tip toes to reach one. As she grabbed the glass, she felt her hair fall down onto her back and then heard a small clacking sound behind her. She turned around, looked down, and saw Kim's pick had fallen out of her hair. Upon hitting the floor its hidden blade had released.

She placed the glass down on the countertop and crouched down. She scooped the pick up from the floor and held it in her hands. She flipped it over a few times running her finger over the floral design imprinted on it. She then ran her thumb up and down the thin blade. She had never really looked at it too closely before but it was a truly beautiful piece of craftsmanship, and its functionality as a weapon was remarkable.

A chilling thought then passed through her mind. The weapons the former Pool members attacked them with all had craftsmanship far beyond normal weaponry. Kim's foster parents had given her the pick. Could they all have possibly been made by the same engineer she wondered.

She retracted the blade back into the pick and quickly shook the thought. From her crouched position she rose fast and slammed the back of her head into the bottom of the cabinet she had left open. She dropped the pick, grabbed at her head, and cursed aloud. Grimacing behind clenched teeth, she dropped back down to a knee. Her entire head began throbbing. She shut her eyes and bit down on her bottom lip, letting out a painful cry that echoed through the house. She pulled her hand down from her head checking to ensure she wasn't bleeding. Her hand was clean but she felt a horrible sting from the spot where her head made contact with the cabinet door.

Still rattled, she stared at the wooden floor beneath her, pressing hard against her head. She was sure she would have a knot rise soon. The sting began to wane after a bit but the spot remained tender to the touch. She shut her eyes again and exhaled from out her nose.

"Whoa, careful babe…"

Rin's eyes immediately opened hearing a voice.

"… watch your head, you only get one of those," the voice laughed.

Rin quickly lifted her head and drew back. In front of her stood a girl, and on the girl's face a smile so big, so full, so sweet, it was unnerving. Rin's heart began racing. The girl was unfamiliar, yet she didn't appear to be of any danger to her. She wasn't sure if it was the cheerful tone of her voice, the way she stood so relaxed in front of her with her hands on her hips, or the smile she wore that just wouldn't go away, but somehow she just knew the girl was no threat to her. She could feel it.

Still a bit stunned, Rin stuttered, "Wh-who are you…"

"A friend of your sister."

MAY 18th 1989	Kim is born
JUL 2nd 1989	Colt 45 raids begin
JUL 7th 1989	Kim is separated from her family
NOV 1989	Kim's parents and Rin move east
JAN 1992	The Pool is formed
JAN 10th 1993	Kim(4y/o) is brought to The Home
MAR 1995	Kim(6y/o) is adopted by her foster parents
MAR 2004	Kim's(15y/o) foster parents are murdered
APR 2004	OLD Pool members disband/Crain(18y/o)
JAN 24th 2007	Kim(18y/o) learns of The Pool
MAY 7th 2009	Kim(20y/o) joins The Pool/first kill
JUN 2010	Kim(21y/o) adopts Cindy
APR 2015	Book 1 THE JOY CITY POOL
OCT 2015	Book 2 CHASING GHOSTS
DEC 2015	Book 3 SMOKE & MIRRORS
JAN 2016	Crain seeks out OLD Pool members
MAY 2019	Book 4 THE EPILOGUE

THE JOY CITY POOL
series timeline

Acknowledgements

I would like to dedicate the following page(s) to thank those that motivated me to keep writing, take a chance on my work, and push for publication. The following individuals were sent or given small excerpts of my work (not necessarily this one) and encouraged me to keep writing whether through their praise or constructive criticism.

Names listed in alphabetical order

Alexis Bright
Aliyah C.
Anna Thompson
Averry Cox
Ayana Reynolds
Brianna Watters
Britney Reynolds
Claire K.
Crane O'Hanlon
David L. Hawks
Erin Elledge
Hannah B. Brennan
Hannah Mokulis
Hephzibah Eniade
Hope Anderson
Izabella N. Vital

Kaliya Williams
Kelsee Piercy
Mackenzie Jolene & the entire Monahan family
Melissa Baez
Nichelle Dew
Nicole Nina Náray
Noor Khalid
Olivia Stephens
Peter Revel-Walsh
Rachel Grace Pigott
Regena Dossett
Romae Jarrett
Star Box
Tyson Hills
Whitney McMahan

I owe a special thanks to Vivien Reis, Jenna Moreci, and Bethany Atazadeh for the tips, advice, and coaching they provided via their Youtube channels. Without you three I could not have become the writer that I am today and the care of which this book was handled from start to finish resulting in the finished product would not be nearly as evident without the many teachings and guidance I received from each of you. Thank you all tremendously.

I owe a huge amount of gratitude to Mrs. Berkleigh Cirilli, one of my beta readers and the teacher who gave me the homework assignment that led to me finding my love for writing. Had it not been for you I probably would have never taken writing seriously and I would have never ended up discovering my love for storytelling. You were the first person to show belief in my writing ability and it means the world to me. Without you, not a word of any short story, novel, or narrative I have ever written would exist. As I have told you many times before I will never forget you, and thank you for everything.

A huge thanks to Zane Alexander for being one of my beta readers and assisting in marketing and exposure of my works. I really appreciate the encouragement and feedback you provided that ultimately let me know my work was good enough to be published. Your creativity and storytelling ability you showcase within your own works inspired me to push myself as I attempted to bring my works to life. And so, I absolutely must thank you for your contributions to this book's existence you may not have even known you made. Thank you Zane.

I must thank Samantha Dambach for all the help and resources she supplied me with to help transition my work from an idea in my head, to a word document on my laptop, to an eventual tangible book. Thank you so much for all the wisdom and knowledge you shared with me on the processes of writing, editing, and publishing. Know this book would not and could not exist today without your help.

To my amazing editor, Michelle Krueger, thank you so so so much. The editing process was something that initially terrified me and though we had some hiccups and slowdowns due to factors far out of either of our control we got through it together and ended up with a fantastic final copy of the book and I cannot thank you enough for that. Your edits, proofing, suggestions, praises, and criticisms were all immensely crucial in the polishing of this book and ultimately me achieving my dream of becoming a published author. Wherever it goes, know "The Joy City Pool" would not and could not be what it is today without you and your contributions to it. Thank you for everything.

Massive amount of thanks to Haze Long for bringing this book's front and back cover art to life. When I first sent you the front cover concept sketch that I did in color pencil I thought the cover would look pretty good but you and your talents made the cover truly great. Then you blew me away again with your incredible execution of the back cover. Looking over the finished product never ceases to amaze me and I'm truly honored to have pieces of your original artwork as my book's cover art. Thank you so much Haze.

Big thanks to Sharon Bailey who narrated the audiobook version of this work. Having the book be widely accessible in many different formats was important to me and so I thank you for lending your talents in helping me accomplish this as well as helping with last bit of polishing/editing of the manuscript.

And of course, I must thank my entire family for the love and support they showed me throughout the entire writing and publishing process.

I can't thank you all enough for the time and effort you sacrificed in contributing to this work. All the things each and every one of you did, told me you loved about my work, or told me you didn't like so much were considered and played a pivotal role in what the final product is today. I hope as you read you were able to take pride in knowing you contributed to this work in one way or another.

Finally, I want to thank any and all who picked up this novel and read it cover to cover. I truly hope you enjoyed your read.

Contact and Social Information

 joycitycontact@gmail.com

 @EverythingJoyCity

 @Everything_JC

 @everythingjoycity

CPSIA information can be obtained
at www.ICGtesting.com
Printed in the USA
BVHW032249200423
662743BV00005B/103